D1562929

Exploration of Ancient Key-Dweller Remains on the Gulf Coast of Florida

Frank Hamilton Cushing

Introduction to the 2000 edition by Randolph J. Widmer
Foreword by Jerald T. Milanich, Series Editor

University Press of Florida

Gainesville/Tallahassee/Tampa/Boca Raton

Pensacola/Orlando/Miami/Jacksonville

Foreword and introduction copyright 2000 by the Board of Regents of the State of Florida
First published in 1896 by the American Philosophical Society, *Proceedings*, vol. 35, no. 153;
reprinted 1897
Printed in the United States of America on acid-free paper

05 04 03 02 01 00 6 5 4 3 2 1

Library of Congress Cataloging-in-Publication Data
Cushing, Frank Hamilton, 1857–1900.
Exploration of ancient key-dweller remains on the gulf coast of Florida / Frank Hamilton
Cushing; introduction to the 2000 edition by Randolph J. Widmer;
foreword by Jerald T. Milanich.
p. cm.–(Southeastern classics in archaeology, anthropology, and history)
"First published in 1896 by the American Philosophical Society, Proceedings,
vol. 35, no. 153"–T.p. verso.
Includes bibliographical references.
ISBN 0-8130-1791-2 (acid-free paper)
1. Indians of North America–Florida–Gulf Coast–Antiquities.
2. Gulf Coast (Fla.)–Antiquities. I.Title. II. Series.
E78.F6 C87 2000
975.9'00497–dc21   99-089305

The University Press of Florida is the scholarly publishing agency for the State University System
of Florida, comprising Florida A&M University, Florida Atlantic University, Florida International
University, Florida State University, University of Central Florida, University of Florida,
University of North Florida, University of South Florida, and University of West Florida.

University Press of Florida
15 Northwest 15th Street
Gainesville, FL 32611
http://www.upf.com

Contents

Foreword

What makes a classic? Why are some books and articles as useful today as when they were first written? For archaeologists, anthropologists, and historians interested in the Native American cultures of the southeastern United States and the events of the colonial period, classics are references that contain ideas and knowledge essential to research. Some classics have helped to shape a field of study, others helped in the development of the fundamental taxonomies in use today, and still others offer basic building blocks of information that can be used to create theoretical models. Many classics exhibit all of these characteristics. These are indeed publications that active researchers need and use.

On my shelves there are a number of classics that I consult frequently. My students covet them, and I guard them zealously, for scholarly as well as financial reasons. Classics—if one can still find them at all—can cost a pretty penny!

The knowledge published in classics endures through the ages, but the physical books themselves are often less fortunate. Originally published in paperback with non-acid-free pages and bindings, in limited printings or in hard-to-find journals, some of them have become rare indeed.

The Southeastern Classics series puts back into print books and articles deemed by scholars to be timeless treasures, resources that we all use but that are difficult or impossible to find. As someone who has always loved books and could not wait for the Bookmobile to visit my neighborhood during the summers of my youth, I am very pleased to be a part of this project.

Frank Hamilton Cushing's report on the Key Marco site on Florida's Gulf of Mexico coast is a classic by anyone's standards. At Key Marco in the late nineteenth century, Frank Cushing, a sometimes controversial figure, made archaeological discoveries that have never been duplicated. Most important, he promptly issued a well-illustrated monograph documenting those discoveries for all time.

Today the artifacts he recovered are also available for study, curated at the University Museum of the University of Pennsylvania, the Smithsonian Institution's National Museum of the Natural History, and the Florida Museum of Natural History in Gainesville. Cushing made certain that the past would be preserved for the future.

This facsimile reprint of Cushing's monograph *Exploration of Ancient Key-Dweller Remains on the Gulf Coast of Florida* (originally published in 1896 and reprinted in 1897) includes a new introduction by Randolph J. Widmer of the

University of Houston. He is no stranger to the Key Marco site, having carried out excavations there in 1995, 1998, and 1999. I have long admired Randolph Widmer, whose contributions to our understanding of the archaeology of southwest Florida are substantial. His introduction places Cushing and Key Marco in the context of their time and highlights their present status as archaeological classics.

I would be remiss if I did not mention the ongoing southwest Florida archaeology project of my colleague William H. Marquardt. Building on the work of Frank Cushing and Randolph Widmer and supported in large part by the Calusa Constituency, an organization of private citizens, William Marquardt and his team are uncovering new information about the Calusa Indians of that coastal region, their precolumbian ancestors, and the environment in which those native people lived. They also are giving that information back to the public through a variety of educational programs. Were Frank Hamilton Cushing alive today, I am certain he would be counted among the members of the Calusa Constituency.

Jerald T. Milanich
Series Editor

Introduction

RANDOLPH J. WIDMER

Florida has been fortunate in having had a number of famous anthropologists who, although not primarily archaeologists, directed archaeological projects in the state. They include Julian Steward, considered the founder of the ecological approach in anthropology, who directed excavation at the Surfside site on Miami Beach (Willey 1949); Aleš Hrdlička, founder of the American Association of Physical Anthropologists, who conducted an extensive archaeological survey of the Ten Thousand Islands (Hrdlička 1922); and Frank Hamilton Cushing, regarded as the father of American ethnography (Haviland 1998), who conducted archaeological surveys and excavations along the southwest Florida coast. Cushing's research caught the attention of the world's archaeological community in the last years of the nineteenth century.

In the spring of 1896, Frank Hamilton Cushing conducted one of the most remarkable excavations in the annals of American archaeology on a small shell key located just north of Marco Island in what was then Lee County, Florida. This small island was called Key Marco, and for almost 100 years it has been all but forgotten as a place-name and as an archaeological site. After Lee County was divided, the site's location became Collier County.

A tourist visiting Marco Island today and asking about the location of Key Marco would be directed to an island just south of Marco Island, originally named Horr's Island but renamed Key Marco by its developers, presumably because of the negative connotation of the phonetic pronunciation of the name and the effect it might have on real estate sales. Increasing the confusion, the late nineteenth-century settlers of Key Marco referred to the island as Marco Village, and in 1927 the name was officially changed to Collier City (Coleman 1995:18). Today the Key Marco of 1896 is referred to as Old Marco Village. To add to the muddle, anthropologist Marion Gilliland erroneously labeled Marco Island "Key Marco" and had the site vaguely labeled on her published map so that it straddled both the site and a peninsula opposite Collier Bay west of the actual site location (Gilliland 1975:8, fig. 1). In spite of all of these variations in nomenclature, the Key Marco site persisted through time.

Two archaeological site numbers have been assigned for the Key Marco site: 8Cr49 (8 for Florida, Cr for Collier County, 49 for the forty-ninth site in Collier County), used exclusively for the excavations in the "Court of the Pile Dwellers" by Cushing and those before him; and 8Cr48, used to designate all the other excavated area and the surface collection made from the large Key Marco site as mapped by Wells Sawyer, Cushing's artist and surveyor, in 1896. Later projects in the latter area would include the testing of John and Linda Van Beck (1965) and my own operations on the site (Widmer 1996).

Key Marco is no longer an island but a peninsula, having been joined with Marco Island by dredge-and-fill operations that culminated in the mid-1960s. The site has been leveled to a more or less uniform elevation, with the original shell mounds pushed over to fill in the low-lying swales and make way for development. This process was observed as early as 1918 (Hrdlička 1922).

Today it is impossible to visualize the original topography. The site has houses, condominiums, shops, and restaurants on its now-level surface, which is dissected by canals and paved streets. There is nothing visible to suggest an aboriginal site, and only the Olde Marco Inn, which dates from 1883, is there to remind us of the pioneer settlement that once occupied the site. Yet just beneath the houses on lots 7, 8, and 9 on Vernon Place lies the location of the Court of the Pile Dwellers, a small muck pond less than an acre in size, which in 1896 made this site one of the most important in the world.

The reason for this fame was the spectacular collection of wooden artifacts recovered from the pond. The recovery was remarkable because the site is located in a tropical area, perhaps the least likely area in the United States for the survival of such artifacts, which had been preserved by the high concentration of anaerobic muck and peat in the pond. Even more remarkable, none of the explorers were professional archaeologists with university degrees. Perhaps it was this situation that made the expedition so celebrated and the envy of all archaeologists of the time. They had been "scooped" by outsiders! This created a contentious atmosphere that has clouded the Key Marco excavations to this day. I daresay no other important archaeological site in the United States has so controversial and fuzzy a history.

The story of the expedition is dramatic and filled with tension. The project was constantly on the brink of failure and disaster. Ultimately, it never lived up to its potential. The collections resulting from the project were fought over, divided, and dispersed to different institutions, and Cushing, its brilliant director, met an untimely death only four years after the excavation.

The very existence of the Key Marco expedition was the result of a fortuitous coincidence. Lieutenant Colonel Charles Durnford, a retired British military officer, world traveler, and amateur antiquarian, was exploring ancient canals and mounds in nearby Naples when he heard of some wooden artifacts dug up by Captain William D. Collier in a muck pond on his property just to the south of Key Marco. Durnford made several excavations of his own there and recovered wooden artifacts, including a carved animal head. He brought them to the Museum of the University of Pennsylvania. (Later they were deposited in the British Museum [Snapp 1996].) He chose this museum because he had earlier met the curator of the American section of the University of Pennsylvania Archaeology Department, Henry Mercer, in Europe. By coincidence, Frank Cushing was in

Philadelphia on sick leave from the Bureau of American Ethnology in Washington. He was under the care of a physician, Dr. William Pepper, who was also president of the university's Archaeology Department. Everyone recognized the importance of the discovery, and Cushing immediately volunteered to direct the excavation on Collier's property. He received a leave from the Bureau of Ethnology, and the adventure began. The expedition was named after Dr. Pepper and Phebe A. Hearst (wife of publisher William Randolph Hearst), who provided funding.

I never cease to be amazed by the lucky coincidence of this initial meeting of individuals and the final selection of the expedition team. What if Cushing had not been ill and had never come to Philadelphia? What if Clarence B. Moore, a local Philadelphia archaeologist of considerable renown (albeit at a competitive institution, the Philadelphia Academy of Natural Science), had been called in to view the artifacts and put in charge of the excavations? What if Durnford had gone to that museum instead of the one at the University of Pennsylvania? Clarence B. Moore must surely have wished to have been put in charge of the expedition. We know this because after Cushing's excavation of the muck pond on Key Marco, Moore visited the muck pond site and others in the vicinity and made his own excavations and investigations on four occasions, in 1900, 1904, 1906, and 1907 (Moore 1900, 1905, 1907). Not one of his visits resulted in finds even remotely similar to Cushing's, yet only after the fourth failed attempt did he write off the possibility of duplicating Cushing's find.

Cushing had asserted that the find was fortuitous and not likely to be replicated in the area. But Moore did not heed Cushing's assertion, a situation all too common in Moore's work. Unlike Cushing, he was not impressed with the archaeological potential of southwest Florida; he was not an anthropologist but an antiquarian, interested in finding ceramic vessels and similar objects. His evaluation of the region after four trips there was less than enthusiastic.

> Our own experience and that of others has convinced us that in the shell-heaps of the southwest Florida coast, which extend southward from above Cedar Key, practically nothing of interest has been found that can compensate one for the heavy outlay of time and money needed for their demolition.
>
> An accurate survey of the shell site on Turner River might be of interest, but it is our belief that digging into the shell deposits hereafter will be more frequently suggested than done. (Moore 1919:401)

It is impossible to overestimate the importance of Cushing's work to the archaeology of southwest Florida. I vividly remember discussing this situation with the late John W. Griffin, the dean of south Florida archaeology, who had spent much of his career refining and explaining the archaeology of this area. We both ponedered the same question: What would scholars have thought of the archaeology of southwest Florida if Cushing had not made his remarkable discoveries or if there were no firsthand Spanish archival sources for the area? Our conclusion was that archaeologists would consider the sites and remains of the south-west Florida coast as simply the midden accumulations of nomadic foragers at a basic level of sociopolitical organization, when in fact they represent one of the most complex societies encountered by the Spanish explorers in the United States.

Cushing's excavations of the Court of the Pile Dwellers gave us material evidence of this complexity. Along with the Spanish accounts of the area, those excavations highlighted the importance of this region in the study of the precolumbian United States. But even so, southwest Florida long remained a forgotten chapter in the annals of American archaeology. To me, this is one of the great puzzles of archaeology. Not until the 1980s did archaeologists once again focus on the southwest Florida coast.

Philip Phillips, in an introduction to an earlier reprint edition of the Key Marco monograph, admonishes Cushing for his flowery, dramatic writing style, his quick intuitive speculations, and his hyperbole over measurements of the heights of mounds. He adds that Cushing's genius is not as an archaeologist but instead as a writer of fiction (Phillips 1973:xv). Phillips could not be more in error. He obviously has never visited Mound Key in Estero Bay. If he had, he would have realized how brilliantly and accurately Cushing's description captures the character of the site, if not its precise dimensions. Cushing's knowledge of anthropology was far beyond that of contemporary archaeologists such as Clarence B. Moore, William H. Holmes, and Cyrus Thomas. His approach to archaeology—his legacy to the field—turns out to be more modern than that of other archaeologists like Phillips who were primarily concerned with artifact styles and archaeological classification, not with people. Cushing was the first true anthropological archaeologist in this country and should be thought of as the founder of American anthropological archaeology. But his contributions to the discipline of archaeology go beyond even that. He should be considered the father of modern archaeological fieldwork in the United States.

Who was this man and how did he come to be the genius that he was? Frank Hamilton Cushing was born on July 22, 1857, in Erie County, Pennsylvania. He was a sickly child, and his poor health was to plague him throughout his short but intense life. It prevented him from rough play with other children, so he would often wander alone through the woods close to his house near Barre Center, in Orleans County, New York. He became a keen observer of nature and found his first projectile point at the age of ten.

In 1870 his family moved to Medina, New York, a move that seems to have stimulated his interest in archaeology by exposing him to archaeological finds of the time (some of which, like the Cardiff Giant, were bogus). He also met people who were knowledgeable about and interested in archaeology. He built a hut on an Indian village site and began collecting artifacts, analyzing and replicating them to determine how they were made and what their function was. He sought out experts wherever he could to help him learn more about artifacts and archaeology. At the age of seventeen, he submitted a report on his artifact collection from Orleans County to the Smithsonian Institution, and it was published in the Smithsonian's annual review (Gilliland 1989:26).

Cushing became obsessed with learning as much as possible about archaeology and wrote to the Smithsonian begging for more information. During a visit to Cornell University, he so impressed a professor of geology with his ability to make an impromptu collection of artifacts right on the campus that he was offered free admission to the university to pursue his interests in archaeology. He left Cornell after a year to take a position at the Smithsonian in 1875, where, at the age of nineteen, he was made curator of the Department of Ethnology of the National Museum (Gilliland 1989:26). His first duty was the preparation of artifact collections for the upcoming Centennial Exposition in Philadelphia. He accompanied the collection to Philadelphia and during his six months there met many archaeologists from other parts of the United States. He achieved all of this without formal university training, having learned archaeology on his own by reading and by talking with as many professionals as he could.

His early interest in archaeology led Cushing to gather numerous collections of artifacts, and he was skilled at replicating aboriginal tools and artifacts. His manual dexterity was so astonishing that the ethnologist W. J. McGee called him a "manual genius." John Wesley Powell, the founder and first director of the Bureau of American Ethnology, later maintained that Cushing could make any Zuni Indian tool better than the Zuni themselves could.

In 1879, at the age of twenty-two, Cushing went to the southwestern United States. This trip forever changed his perspective on archaeology and gave him a unique intellectual advantage that no other American archaeologist possessed. Unfortunately the experience was a two-edged sword: It provided him with insights and inspiration, but his already poor health was severely compromised. The health conditions among the Zuni Indians ultimately led to his early death.

For four and a half years Cushing was totally immersed in Zuni culture, cut off for the most part from the outside world. He lived as they did, eating their meals, living in their homes, wearing their clothes, and performing the everyday activities of an adult male. He learned their language and was instructed in their religion, myths, and rituals. He was even initiated into the Zuni Bow Priesthood, and became an honorary chief, with the added rank of Warrior of the Cacique. Cushing learned and understood the complex organization of Zuni society as no non-Indian had before him (Basso 1979:14).

This ethnographic experience provided him with the means to break out of the antiquarian mold and to go beyond the cultural-historical and functional concerns of American archaeology at the time and address processual problems. Cushing was many years ahead of his time with respect to his archaeological interpretations. How was this possible, and why were there not others to champion his cause? The answer lies in the very experience that gave him these insights.

Cushing became an ethnographer and was the first non-Indian to immerse himself in an American Indian culture for the express purpose of learning about that culture, of experiencing and participating in Indian life firsthand. He could relate to Zunis as a fellow Zuni with local knowledge rather merely an educated observer with the prevailing Victorian mindset of his culture. When he interpreted the archaeological record, it was from an experience that could not be duplicated by contemporary archaeologist. With this newfound perspective, Cushing had a methodology and the background for breaking away from the direct-historical approach common at the time. The insights and perspective he gained living with the Zuni were more useful in interpreting and reconstructing the past than sketchy ethnohistoric accounts. Not that he ignored the latter—he clearly did not. But he saw the advantage of placing the archaeological record in an ethnographic context. It is of even greater importance that he did his ethnography in Zuni prior to the two major archaeological projects he conducted.

Cushing's first project was the Hemenway Expedition to the Hohokam region of southern Arizona. Here he could use his ethnographic knowledge of the Zuni as a framework for the direct-historical approach. But on his second major expedition—Pepper-Hearst, the report of which is presented here—he could not use the ethnographic knowledge of the Zuni in a direct-historical approach since the two areas (the southwest United States and southwest Florida) were not linked historically. In Florida he had to utilize a base of ethnographic knowledge as analogy. He reasoned that if he had used the Zuni as ethnographic models in Arizona, why could he not use other cultures in Florida that might be similar in other features? That is exactly what he did, and it is the reason for the success of his interpretations and reconstructions regarding Key Marco.

Another advantage that Cushing had over the archaeologists of his time was his understanding of the social and political organization of an Indian culture. True, that knowledge applied only to the Zuni, but it gave him a perspective that other scholars of the time did not have. His experience with Zuni life gave him insight into all aspects of their culture and allowed him to see archaeological cultures in the same way. Thus he was able to utilize cross-cultural knowledge of the Zuni to interpret and reconstruct the prehistoric culture of southwest Florida. Moreover, he could see the advantage of using ethnographic parallels from other cultures as well. This was not done by any other archaeologist.

Cushing was on track to be the preeminent American archaeologist of his time, but this was not to be the case. Instead, most experts would award William H. Holmes or Cyrus Thomas that distinction. Holmes was a pioneer in the study of artifact technology and use, but he never went on to focus on entire cultures. Thomas did a masterful job of synthesizing the existing archaeological data of the eastern United States to address the age-old question regarding the origin of the mound builders. His conclusions were that ancestors of the Indians of the eastern United States indeed constructed the mounds. As such, it was one of the first problem-oriented, large-scale archaeological projects in the country—but it was by no means the first. That honor belongs to Cushing for his Hemenway Expedition (Haury 1970).

Neither Holmes nor Thomas made systematic attempts to obtain the artifacts for study. Holmes utilized "field agents" to scour the countryside to obtain artifacts, but there was little concern regarding how these artifacts were unearthed from the ground. He conducted stratigraphic trenching of quarry sites on the Potomac and published detailed stratigraphic profiles of the trenches (Holmes 1897). He even mapped features of debitage together with the anvil on which it was fractured. While he did outline the stratigraphy of the site, there was no attempt to use the provenience information in the study of the artifacts. Furthermore, the excavations were made not in a habitation site but rather in a resource extraction site. Holmes's archaeology did not measure up to that of Cushing.

The irony is that Cushing was not exclusively an archaeologist. In his four and a half years among the Zuni he had become an accomplished ethnographer and, as such, identifiable as a cultural anthropologist as well as an archaeologist. Such dual specialties were not uncommon. In the late nineteenth century anthropology was in its infancy and not really defined as a discipline divided into subdisciplines (such as physical anthropology, linguistic anthropology, cultural anthropology, and archaeology), as it is today. It was not unheard of for a single individual to work and publish in archaeology, ethnography, physical anthropology, and linguistics. Even so, Cushing's ethnographic research was so important that I wonder how many cultural anthropologists even know he did archaeology! Fortunately for us he did and did it well.

Cushing's brilliance is differentially appreciated by archaeologists then and now. More and more contemporary archaeologists are astonished by his insights and analysis, but he has not yet been accorded the place in the history of American archaeology that he truly deserves. For example, in *A History of American Archaeology*, there is only a single passage about him: "Frank Hamilton Cushing, the leader of the privately sponsored Hemenway Expedition, helped pioneer the direct-historical approach in the Southwest and combined both ethnography and archaeology in his work" (Willey and Sabloff 1980:51). In *A History of Archaeological Thought*, Bruce Trigger has only a single sentence about Cushing, and it is shared with another archaeologist! "Archeologists such as Frank Cushing (1857–1900) and J. W. Fewkes (1850–1930), in their studies of the Pueblo Indians of the southwestern United States, paid much attention to determining by means of careful ethnographic parallels what prehistoric artifacts had been used for and how they had been made" (1989:124).

Some archaeologists, however, have appreciated his contributions to anthropology. Emil W. Haury has paid tribute to the Hemenway Expedition: "In retrospect, Cushing's work must be acknowledged as the first well-organized, expertly staffed, and abundantly financed effort to understand the prehistory of the then little-known southwestern United States" (1970:3). The noted Maya archaeologist William Haviland dedicates his introductory text in cultural anthropology to him (Haviland 1998), but it is probably more for his contribution as an ethnographer than as an archaeologist.

Why has Cushing not received the credit that he is due? I offer three, possibly four, reasons. First, he did not have a college degree. He was self-educated and therefore not considered on an equal footing with contemporary academics (though he certainly found favor with his employers). Second, he did not publish much—only a single 45-page preliminary publication on the Hemenway

Expedition (Cushing 1890) and the present volume, first published in 1896. In professional archaeology, accomplishments are based on publications, and Cushing's are sparse. Surprisingly, when he is mentioned in the history of American archaeology it is always in regard to his work in the Southwest, never the Pepper-Hearst Expedition. There is no good reason for this omission unless the publication was simply too difficult to obtain.

The third reason is partly responsible for his lack of publications. Cushing was in poor health, and most of his time out of the field was spent recuperating from illness rather than writing. It is hard to believe that the photograph in Marion Gilliland's *Key Marco's Buried Treasure* (1989) is of a man probably in his thirties. Unfortunately, his untimely death in 1900 at the age of forty-three, just four years after the Key Marco excavation, put a tragic end to the work on the site collection and, more important, to his publication record.

I offer a fourth reason, highly speculative, for his absence from the history of American archaeology: He was ahead of his time, and his work at Key Marco could not be readily placed in the archaeological periods in American archaeology.

If I were asked to select one archaeological expedition as the basis for a Hollywood movie, it would without a doubt be the remarkable chronicle of Cushing's Key Marco expedition. No writer could create a screenplay as suspenseful and exotic as what really happened in the Pepper-Hearst Expedition. What occurs in the pages that follow is the story of the most remarkable archaeological odyssey in the United States.

At the end of the nineteenth century the Key Marco site was located in the most inhospitable region of what was then the United States. It was impossible to get to southwest Florida by land because there were no roads connected to the region. Travel by boat, though costly, dangerous, and in this instance untimely, was the only way to reach to the area. Indeed, Cushing's expedition was delayed when the team had to wait for their boat, the *Silver Spray*, to finish an earlier mission. Then it ran aground, causing even greater delay and loss of time and money (Gilliland 1989:67). Cushing took advantage of this delay to excavate the Stafford mound near Tarpon Springs, Florida. Eventually, he made his way to Key Marco to begin the most important archaeological excavation yet conducted in the United States.

Three individuals were responsible for the success of the expedition: Cushing, Wells Sawyer, and Carl Bergmann. This highly talented, interdisciplinary team, probably the first of its kind in the eastern United States, ensured the success of the Key Marco excavation.

Wells M. Sawyer was the project artist and photographer, At the time, Sawyer was an illustrator for the United States Geological Survey and was on loan to the expedition. Without his spectacular watercolor renditions of the fragile wooden artifacts, much of the information from the masks and from other carved and painted artifacts would have been lost. Once the wooden artifacts were exposed, the paint began to fade and disappear before one's very eyes. Sawyer captured the painted designs on these masterpieces with black-and-white photographs and watercolor paintings. This latter form of recording artifacts was essential in the days before color photography in order to capture not only the colors but also the subtleties of the design and its execution.

Sawyer was also the expedition's surveyor and prepared a precise topographic map of the Key Marco site with one-foot contour intervals. Although Cushing was in error with regard to the heights of mounds in the Charlotte Harbor–Pine Island Sound region (also reported in the present volume), there is no such exaggeration in the Key Marco site map prepared by Sawyer. A mound excavated by the Van Becks (1965), who did not realize it was actually on Key Marco, has now been located on Sawyer's contour map. They measured the mound as 15 feet above sea level, the exact elevation indicated on Sawyer's map. The same holds true for a mound near the Olde Marco Inn that I excavated in 1998; the elevation as I measured it matches the elevation on Sawyer's topographic map. Thus we have independent confirmation of the accuracy of Sawyer's map.

Sawyer's attention to detail and his fabulous skill as an artist, draftsman, photographer, and surveyor were invaluable contributions to the expedition. He also took notes (Gilliland 1989:59). When the project ended, Sawyer went on to become an influential and important American artist specializing in watercolors. Some of his watercolors are beautiful scenes from Key Marco, which he painted at the end of the day (Gilliland 1989:59). Unlike Cushing, Sawyer was blessed with good health and lived into his nineties.

The last—and least appreciated—member of the expedition and the one to whom we should be most grateful is also the least well known. He is Carl F. W. Bergmann, the preparer and conservator of the artifacts. Many of the wooden artifacts from Key Marco are in a remarkable state of preservation, surely attributable to careful handling, cleaning, preparation, and preservation. This is even more impressive considering that artifact conservation was then in its infancy. The only hint at the method of conservation used refers to the packing of the wooden artifacts in sand so that they would not dry out too fast (Cushing, cited in Gilliland 1989:88).

What makes Cushing's work at Key Marco so important? Was anything that he did really revolutionary in its approach to the past? Did it result in any breakthroughs in our understanding of the archaeology of southwest Florida? The answer to these questions is a resounding affirmative. In my opinion, Cushing made several groundbreaking contributions to archaeological interpretation, method, and theory. As noted above, he was the first American archaeologist who made a systematic attempt to interpret artifacts and archaeology from a cross-cultural, ethnographic perspective, though he was severely criticized by his contemporaries for it. He drew upon cultural analogs from varying locations in the world, including Venezuela, Polynesia, and the southwestern United States. This method simply was not used at the time; rather, the direct-historical approach was the standard. It was not until the 1960s and 1970s that cross-cultural ethnographic data were used in archaeology in the United States.

Cushing was also the first American archaeologist who actually interpreted the artifacts recovered from an excavation in sociocultural behavioral terms, not simply artifact function. This was of course because he was an ethnographer as well as an archaeologist. His ethnographic experience at Zuni gave an anthropological perspective to his work that differed from that of an art historian or of a collector. I believe this is the reason many of his colleagues disapproved of his work—along with their jealousy, provoked by his finds. Even the "whole pot"-jaded Clarence Moore went to south Florida to try and replicate Cushing's finds (Moore 1900, 1905, 1907)—not once or twice, but four times! That is a clear indication of how important Cushing's finds were considered in their day. Most contemporary archaeologists, most notably Moore, were still trying to get fancy artifacts for museums. The focus in archaeology at the time was on figuring out time and space systematics of the artifacts, how they were made, and what their immediate function was. Instead Cushing was using the artifacts to try to interpret the social, political, and religious contexts of a prehistoric culture. Even more amazing, he actually attempted to explain the emergence of the sociopolitical complexity that he excavated at Key Marco. It was not until the late 1960s that American archaeologists began using this approach on a routine basis—the processual archaeological movement that continues today.

Another reason that the excavation at the Court of the Pile Dwellers was so important is the incredible range of organic artifacts recovered from the site. No other site in the southeastern United States has produced as many wooden and perishable cord artifacts as did the Key Marco site, particularly from such a wide range of functions, including utilitarian, subsistence extraction, sociopolitical, and religious. This collection provides a unique baseline for fleshing out the potential range of wooden artifacts likely to be encountered at other archaeological sites of similar sociopolitical complexity in the southeastern United States.

Cushing also made important contributions to archaeological field methods. He was the first archaeologist to use a grid system; at Key Marco it consisted of conjoining 10-by-10-foot squares. He numbered these squares sequentially from top to bottom, left to right; there are 81 in the Court of the Pile Dwellers. On this grid, he even mapped the locations of previous excavations made by himself, Durnford, Collier, and Wilkins, as well as eight fallen wooden pilings.

He also excavated stratigraphically, separating artifacts by their distinctive layers, and provided the first stratigraphic profile of an archaeological site in southwest Florida. Cushing appears to be the first archaeologist to actually provide the general provenience for each of the illustrated artifacts in this report, thus making it possible to map the artifacts to their original 10-by-10-foot square. (It would be interesting to see if any spatial patterning emerged from such an exercise.)

He was also a pioneer in community pattern studies. He treated archaeological sites as settlements or communities and specifically maintained that the shell sites were intentionally constructed for temples and houses and not simply midden accumulations, even though they are made of shell. My excavations at Key Marco in three different locations (Widmer 1996) and at the Shell Island site, 8Cr55, in Rookery Bay have confirmed his statements.

Cushing also was the first archaeologist to suggest that the structures in southwest Florida were erected on pilings or on piers that extended into the water. Cushing based this conclusion on the fallen pilings that he recorded in his excavation. My initial positive testing of Cushing's idea of pile dwellings came from my work at the Solana site, 8Ch67 (Widmer 1986). Originally, I thought that this site was a specialized plant extraction or processing site in the interior, one that supplied coastal villages. However, upon excavation of the site, I realized it was a coastal fishing site. I remembered Cushing's interpretation of pile structures and used that as a model for testing features I found at the site. Sure enough, they were piling encrustations, indicating that the site was underwater when it was occupied. Subsequent research at the sites at Key Marco and Shell Island (Widmer 1996) has indicated that this is a characteristic settlement pattern rather than an isolated situation. I suspect that most houses in prehistoric southwest Florida were indeed pile dwellings out over water, and it was Cushing who was the first to indicate this finding correctly.

Cushing recognized that the Indians of south Florida spoke a language affiliated structurally with those of northern South America—an astonishingly precocious observation considering that it was not the prevailing theory of the day. Both Brinton and Putnam (Cushing 1896:439 [111]) admonished him for this classification, but it now appears that Cushing may have been correct. Julian Granberry (1993, 1995) has suggested that Timucua and Calusa *are* indeed related to languages of northern South America. Granberry even goes on to suggest that groups from South America migrated to Florida at some time in the prehistoric past—hardly a new idea because it is exactly what Cushing stated.

The hypothesis of a migration or diffusion from South America 3,000 to 4,000 years ago was also proposed by James Ford (1969), who used archaeological evidence instead of linguistic evidence to view an American Formative stage from which complex society in the Americas emerged. A quote by Cushing bears a striking similarity (except stated in slightly more archaic prose) to Ford's concept of the American Formative: "I have ventured to suggest that the resemblance between mound-groups of our own land, and the foundation-groups of ancient Central American cities—the plans for the principal structures of which are so strikingly like even the plans of the earlier key structures—may indicate that these, no less than the mound-groups themselves, were developed (with much else in ancient Central American culture) from an original sea environment of the same kind" (Cushing 1896:445 [117]). Ironically, neither Granberry nor Ford attributed their ideas to Cushing, nor did they cite his work.

Cushing does differ from Ford in one important and more modern perspective. Ford saw the traits of complex culture diffusing from a center in Central America or possibly South America. Although Cushing recognized the diffusion of traits and possibly even language from South America, he did not see this diffusion to be causal in the development of the sociopolitical complexity in southwest Florida. Cushing saw the Key Dweller culture developing independently out of the need to adapt to local environmental conditions, and he stated this view explicitly: "After all, the chief significance of these discoveries and finds of ours in the keys of southwest Florida is to be found, as I have said before, in the unique illustration they afford of a peculiar local development in culture and art as influenced by, or related to, a peculiar environment; and in this, while they may not pertain to a new or hitherto unknown people, they certainly do reveal either a new *phase* of human culture, or else an old culture in an entirely new light" (Cushing 1896:441 [113]). This passage clearly indicates that although Cushing understood that there were cultural influences from other regions, this spread of language, people, and culture traits happened early in the prehistory of the southwest Florida coast, and that the developments which took place were brought about by adjustments to environmental conditions. This is a very modern processual argument that still holds true today. Amazingly, it was written over a century ago.

Cushing was the first to correlate the archaeology at the Key Marco site with a chiefdom level of sociocultural integration—something never done before anywhere in the Americas until 1968. The systematic development of this scheme in archaeology was not reintroduced anywhere until 1968 by William Sanders and Barbara Price in their monumental work *Mesoamerica, the Evolution of a Civilization*. The reintroduction of the term *chiefdom* into the southeastern United States is usually credited to Christopher Peebles and Susan Kus in 1973. Today the term is universally used to refer to the political structure of later prehistoric societies in the southeastern United States.

Cushing's most important and lasting contribution to archaeology is that he was concerned with *explaining* why the Indians of Key Marco had a chiefdom. Not only did he reconstruct the culture as a chiefdom; he then went on to explain why it emerged. More important, we still utilize his explanation today. It is best summarized by a passage from Cushing that I used as the epigraph in my work *The Evolution of the Calusa* (Widmer 1988).

> The development of the key dwellers in this direction, is attested by every key ruin—little or great—built so long ago, yet enduring the storms that have since played havoc with the mainland; is mutely yet even more eloquently attested by every great group of the shell mounds on these keys built for the chief's houses and temples; by every lengthy canal built from materials of slow and laborious accumulation from the depths of the sea. Therefore, to my mind, there can be no question that the executive, rather than the social side of government was developed among these ancient key dwellers to an almost disproportionate degree; to a degree which led not only to the establishment among them of totemic priests and headmen, as among the Pueblos, but to more than this—to the development of a favored class, and of chiefdoms even in civil life little short of regal in power and tenure of office. (Cushing 1896:413 [85])

When I showed this passage to my mentor at Pennsylvania State University, William T. Sanders, and asked him when it was written (without letting him know who wrote it or when), he thought sometime in the early 1970s! This clearly indicates that not only are the artifacts from this site important and unique in the eastern United states, but that the reconstruction of Calusa culture that Cushing provides is still current. This Cushing accomplished without further subsistence, settlement, and ceramic distributions—the tools utilized by contemporary archaeologists to reconstruct the social and political organization of past cultures. More important, the explanation that he provides for the "key dweller" chiefdom is still a valid hypothesis. In other words, Cushing was a century ahead of his time with respect to his practice of archaeology. If Cushing was not an archaeological genius, then there is no such being.

References Cited

Basso, Keith H.
1979   History of Ethnological Research. In *Handbook of North American Indians: Southwest*, 9:14–21. Washington, D.C.: Smithsonian Press.
Coleman, Michael
1995   *Marco Island: Culture and History*. Marco Island, Fla: Marco Island Chamber of Commerce.
Cushing, Frank H.
1890   Preliminary Notes on the Origin, Working Hypotheses and Primary Researches of the Hemenway Expedition. In *Seventh International Congress of Americanists* 151–94.
1896   The Pepper-Hearst Expedition: A Preliminary Report on the Exploration of Ancient Key-Dweller Remains on the Gulf Coast of Florida. In *Proceedings of the American Philosophical Society*, November 6, 1896, vol. 35, no. 153. [The report was reprinted in 1897, and the present volume is a facsimile of the reprint. Page numbers cited in the text in brackets are the reprint page numbers.]
Ford, James A.
1970   *A Comparison of the Formative Cultures of the Americas*. Vol. 11, Smithsonian Contributions to Anthropology. Washington, D.C.: Smithsonian Institution.
Gilliland, Marion S.
1975   *The Material Culture of Key Marco, Florida*. Gainesville: University of Florida Press.
1989   *Key Marco's Buried Treasure: Archaeology and Adventure in the Nineteenth Century*. Gainesville: University of Florida Press.
Granberry, Julian
1993   *A Grammar and Dictionary of the Timucua Language*. Tuscaloosa: University of Alabama Press.
1995   The Position of the Calusa Language in Florida Prehistory. *Florida Anthropologist* 48:156–73.
Haury, Emil W.
1970   *Hohokam: Desert Farmers and Craftsmen, Excavations at Snaketown, 1964–1965*. Tucson: University of Arizona Press.
Haviland, William
1998   *Cultural Anthropology*. 9th ed. New York: Holt, Rinehart, and Winston.

Holmes, William H.
1897   Stone Implements of the Potomac-Chesapeake Tidewater Province. *Fifteenth Annual Report, Bureau of American Ethnology, 1893–1894*, 13–152.

Hrdlička, Aleš
1922   *The Anthropology of Florida*. DeLand: Florida State Historical Society.

Moore, Clarence B.
1900   Certain Antiquities of the Florida West Coast. *Journal of the Academy of Natural Sciences of Philadelphia* 11:349–94.
1905   Miscellaneous Investigations in Florida. *Journal of the Academy of Natural Sciences of Philadelphia* 13:299–325.
1907   Notes on the Ten Thousand Islands. *Journal of the Academy of Natural Sciences of Philadelphia* 13:458–70.
1919   Notes on the Archaeology of Florida. *American Anthropologist* 21:400–402.

Peebles, Christopher S., and Susan M. Kus
1973   Some Archaeological Correlates of Ranked Society. *American Antiquity* 42:421–48.

Phillips, Philip
1973   Introduction. *Exploration of Ancient Key Dwellers' Remains on the Gulf Coast of Florida*. New York: AMS Press.

Sanders, William T., and Barbara J. Price
1968   *Mesoamerica: The Evolution of a Civilization*. New York: Random House.

Snapp, Annette L.
1996   The Durnford Collection. *Florida Anthropologist* 49:267–73.

Thomas, Cyrus
1894   Report of the Mound Explorations of the Bureau of Ethnology. *Twelfth Annual Report, Bureau of American Ethnology, 1890–1891*, 1–742.

Trigger, Bruce G.
1989   *A History of Archaeological Thought*. Cambridge: Cambridge University Press.

Van Beck, John C., and Linda M. Van Beck
1965   The Marco Midden, Marco Island, Florida. *The Florida Anthropologist* 18:1–20.

Widmer, Randolph J.
1986   *Prehistoric Adaptation at the Solana Site, Charlotte County, Florida*. Tallahassee: Florida Division of Division of Archives, History, and Records Management, Bureau of Archaeological Research.
1988   *The Evolution of the Calusa*. Tuscaloosa: University of Alabama Press.
1996   Recent Excavations at the Key Marco Site, 8Cr48, Collier County, Florida. *The Florida Anthropologist* 49:10–25.

Willey, Gordon R.
1949   *The Archaeology of Southeast Florida*. Publications in Anthropology, no. 42. New Haven: Yale University.

Willey, Gordon R., and Jeremy A. Sabloff
1980   *A History of American Archaeology*. San Francisco: W. H. Freeman and Co.

PEPPER-HEARST EXPEDITION.

A PRELIMINARY REPORT ON THE

EXPLORATION OF ANCIENT KEY-DWELLER REMAINS ON THE GULF COAST OF FLORIDA.

(PLATES XXV-XXXV.)

By FRANK HAMILTON CUSHING.

(Communicated to the American Philosophical Society, November 6, 1896.)

INTRODUCTORY.

Early in the spring of 1895, Captain W. B. Collier, of Key Marco, southwestern Florida, found, while digging garden-muck from one of the little mangrove-swamps (Section 14, Plate XXXI) that occur, like filled-up coves, among the low-lying shell-banks surrounding his shore-island home, several ancient wooden articles and some pieces of netted cordage. He did not recognize as of artificial origin the first found of these objects—so softened were they by decay, so like the water-soaked fragments of rotten timber and rootlets everywhere encountered in the muck. But the twine-like appearance of some of the seeming root-strands that clung to his digging tools, and the discovery, a little later, of a beautifully shaped and highly polished ladle or cup made from the larger portion of a whelk, or conch-shell, led him to believe that the strands were actual cordage, and that a noticeably curious block of wood, which had been sliced through by his spade and cast aside, was really an article fashioned by man.

A few days later, Mr. Charles Wilkins, of Rochester, N. Y., chanced to sail down that way from the little winter resort of Naples, some fifteen miles north of Key Marco, to seek for tarpon, and thus to hear of this find.

Another guest at Naples, a traveler of wide experience and an accomplished scholar withal, Lieutenant Colonel C. D. Durnford, of the British Army, had organized, a few days previously, an amateur expedition to explore an ancient canal and several small burial mounds near by. In this expedition, Mr. Wilkins had joined. He was therefore much interested in what he heard at Marco, and passed a day in digging there on his own account. He found close to the place that had been opened by Captain Collier and his men, other remains, including portions of two wooden cups—one of them somewhat charred—another shell ladle, several pierced conch tool-heads, and a fairly well-preserved animal figure-head of carved wood. When told by him of these finds, Colonel Durnford, accompanied by his courageous wife, immediately set forth for Marco. He had two small excavations made (in Sections 32, 33, Plate XXXI) as close to those that had previously been made as was possible—for these holes were now flooded with water. Therein, he found a piece of rope, more netting, fragments of gourd-shell, a couple of well-worked little blocks, and a tray of wood, some pegs fastened together with string, two billets, what he regarded as remnants of a "fish-bone necklace," and a neatly pierced bivalve shell.

His antiquarian curiosity regarding these things was thoroughly aroused. But believing them to be the remains possibly of some old-time wreckage, or more probably of some casual deposit made by ancient fishermen and never recovered, and finding work in the water-soaked, foul-smelling muck most difficult to pursue, he discontinued his researches on the second day. In order, however, to ascertain whether the relics he had secured and in part brought away were historic or prehistoric— that is of the Spanish or of a purely aboriginal period—he called at the Museum of the University of Pennsylvania, when passing through Philadelphia some weeks later, to see the Curator of the American Section of the Archæological Department, Mr. Henry C. Mercer, whom he had met in southern Europe a year or two previously. Mr. Mercer was absent, but it chanced that during the same hour, I, too, called at the Museum to pay a brief visit to my friend there, the Director, Mr. Stewart Culin. Thus I was so fortunate as to hear Colonel Durnford's account of the finds. I was also privileged to accompany the President of the Department, Dr. William Pepper (for I was at the time on sick-leave and under his care), when, in response to a courteous note of invitation, he called on Colonel and Mrs. Durnford, at the Bellevue Hotel. With him I saw some of the Marco relics, the piece of rope, the tray and one of the worked blocks or billets of wood. I observed that the rope had been slightly charred at one point, and that the billet was an unfinished object. This, with Colonel Durnford's remarkably clear memoranda and description of the place whence these relics had been derived, led me to infer that it, the place, was not of an isolated character. The relics themselves were indubitably Indian and pre-Columbian. To me they evidenced remote aboriginal occupation, residence that is of the actual site in which they had been found, rather than of merely the neighboring shell-banks. I believed, indeed, that their condition and their occurrence beneath the peaty deposits of muck might even betoken some such phase of life in southern Florida as that of the Ancient Lake Dwellers of Switzerland, or of the Pile and Platform Builders of the Gulf of Maracaibo or the Bayous of the Orinoco in Venezuela.

I, therefore, did not hesitate to assure Dr. Pepper and Col. Durnford of my opinion that the find to which he had drawn our attention would, if fully enough followed up, lead to the most important archæological discovery yet made on any of our coasts. Dr. Pepper also attached great significance to the find. He straightway expressed the wish, indeed, that in the interest of the Department he represented, a reconnaissance of the place, as well as of the surrounding region, might immediately be undertaken, with a view to still further explorations another year, in case my conclusions as to the typical nature of the field were thereby borne out. As Mr. Mercer was loath to leave other and pressing work, I eagerly volunteered—health being equal and consent of my Director in the Bureau of American Ethnology, Major J. W. Powell, being granted—to undertake such a reconnaissance. With that rare public spiritedness, instant foresight and promptitude for which he is so distinguished, your honored Vice-President, Dr. Pepper, forthwith provided funds and otherwise arranged for this preliminary survey by me.

Thus, and through the kind offices of the late Hamilton Disston, Esq., and Col. J. M. Kreamer and their associates, I succeeded in securing, from the Clyde Steamship Company and from those courteous gentlemen of Jacksonville, Col. J. K. Leslie and Major Joseph H. Durkee, passes all the way from New York to Jacksonville, and, by way of the St. John's river to Sanford, and thence by rail diagonally down through the pine lands and the tropic lowlands of Florida, and found myself, within less than a fortnight, at the little town of Punta Gorda, near the mouth of Pease river, a deep tidal inlet, on the gulfward side of that State.

FIRST RECONNAISSANCE.

Description of the Ancient Keys or Artificial Shell Islands.

I was not much delayed in securing two men and a little fishing sloop, such as it was, and in sailing forth one glorious evening late in May, with intent to explore as many as possible of the islands and capes of Charlotte harbor, Pine Island Sound, Caloosa Bay and the lower more open coast as far as Marco, some ninety miles away to the southward.

The bright waters of these connected bays and sounds formed a far-reaching and anon wide-spreading, shallow inland sea. It was hemmed in to the westward by a chain of long, narrow, nearly straight, palmetto and forest-clad reefs or islands, just visible on the horizon ; but, as I later learned, all of sand, save only for occasional capes or promontories of shell that here and there jutted forth into the wide mangrove swamps that everywhere closely invested their inner shores. The shores of the opposite mainland and of Pine Island too—which, intervening, hid them for miles—were even more widely skirted by these tangled tidal swamps.

All around, and apparently all over the many islets that darkly dotted the shimmering expanse of this shoreland sea—somewhat as is shown in Plate XXVI—grew also, straightway from the tide-line upward, these clustering deep green mangroves, so closely and evenly that they seemed, when seen from afar, like gigantic clumps of box in some inundated olden garden. They grew so loftily, too, that from the level of the channel near even the largest islets, naught of their inner contours could be seen.

The astonishment I felt, then, on penetrating into the interior of the very first encountered of these thicket-bound islets, may be better imagined than described, when, after wading ankle deep in the slimy and muddy shoals, and then alternately clambering and floundering for a long distance among the wide-reaching interlocked roots of the mangroves—held hip-high above the green weedy tide-wash by myriad ruddy fingers, bended like the legs of centipedes—I dimly beheld, in the sombre depths of this sunless jungle of the waters, a long, nearly straight, but ruinous embankment of piled-up conch-shells. Beyond it were to be seen—as in the illustration given on Plate XXVII,—other banks, less high, not always regular, but forming a maze of distinct enclosures of various sizes and outlines, nearly all of them open a little at either end or at opposite sides, as if for outlet and inlet.

Threading this zone of boggy bins, and leading in toward a more central point, were here and there open ways like channels. They were formed by parallel ridges of shells, increasing in height toward the interior, until at last they merged into a steep, somewhat extended bench, also of shells, and flat on the top like a platform. Here, of course, at the foot of the platform, the channel ended, in a slightly broadened cove like a landing place ; but a graded depression or pathway ascended from it and crossed this bench or platform, leading to, and in turn climbing over, or rather through, another and higher platform a slight distance beyond. In places off to the side on either hand were still more of these platforms, rising terrace-like, but very irregularly, from the enclosures below to the foundations of great, level-topped mounds, which, like worn-out, elongated and truncated pyramids, loftily and imposingly crowned the whole, some of them to a height of nearly thirty feet above the encircling sea.

All this was not by any means plain at first. Except for mere patches a few feet in width, here and there along the steepest slopes, these elevations, and especially the terraces and platforms above the first series, were almost completely shrouded from view under not only a stunted forest of mulberry, papaya, mastich, iron-wood, button-wood, laurel, live oak and other gnarly kinds of trees, mostly evergreen, and all overrun and bound fast together from top to bottom by leafy, tough and thorny vines, and thong-like clinging creepers, but also by a rank tangle below, of grasses, weeds, brambles, cacti, bristling Spanish bayonets and huge spike-leaved century plants, their tall sere flower stalks of former years standing bare and aslant, like spars of storm-beached shipping above this tumultuous sea of verdure.

The utmost heights were, in places, freer ; but even there, grew weeds and creepers and bushes, not a few, and overtopping them all, some of the most fantastic of trees—the trees *par excellence* of the heights of these ancient keys, the so-called gumbo limbos or West Indian birches— bare, skinny, livid, monstrous and crooked of limb, and, compared with surrounding growth, gigantic. To the topmost branches of these weird-looking trees, brilliant red grosbeaks came and went as I climbed. Long ere I saw them, I could hear them trilling, in plaintive flute-like strains, to mates in far-away trees, perhaps on other groups of mounds—whence at least answers like faint echoes of these nearer songs came lonesomely calling back as though across void hollows.

The bare patches along the ascents to the mounds were, like the

ridges below, built up wholly of shells, great conch-shells chiefly, blackened by exposure for ages ; and ringing like thin potsherds when disturbed even by the light feet of the raccoons and little dusky brown rab-
bits that now and then scuttled across them from covert to covert and
that seemed to be, with the ever-present grosbeaks above, and with
many lizards and some few rattlesnakes and other reptiles below, the
principal dwellers on these lonely keys—if swarming insects may be left
unnamed !

But everywhere else it was necessary to cut and tear the way step by
step. Wherever thus revealed, the surface below, like the bare spaces
themselves, proved to be also of shells, smaller or much broken on the
levels and gentler slopes, and mingled with scant black mold on the
wider terraces, as though these had been formed with a view to cultivation and supplied with soil from the rich muck beds below. Here also
occurred occasional potsherds and many worn valves of gigantic clams
and whorls of huge univalves that appeared to have been used as hoes
and picks or other digging tools, and this again suggested the idea that
at least the wider terraces—many of which proved to be not level, but
filled with basin-shaped depressions or bordered by retaining walls—had
been used as garden plats, some, perhaps, as drainage basins. But the
margins of these, whether raised or not, and the edges of even the lesser
terraces, the sides of the graded ways leading up to or through them,
and especially the slopes of the greater mounds, were all of unmixed
shell, in which, as on the barren patches, enormous nearly equal-sized
whelks or conch-shells prevailed.

Such various features, seen one by one, impressed me more and more
forcibly, as indicating general design—a structural origin of at least the
enormous accumulations of shell I was so slowly and painfully travers-
ing, if not, indeed, of the entire key or islet. Still, my mind was not,
perhaps, wholly disabused of the prevalent opinion that these and like
accumulations on capes of the neighboring mainland were primarily stu-
pendous shell heaps, chiefly the undistributed refuse remaining from ages
of intermittent aboriginal occupation, until I had scaled the topmost of
the platforms. Then I could see that the vast pile on which I stood,
and of which the terraces I had climbed were, in a sense, irregular stages,
formed in reality a single, prodigious elbow-shaped foundation, crowned
at its bend by a definite group of lofty, narrow and elongated mounds,
that stretched fan-like across its summit like the thumb and four fingers
of a mighty outspread hand. Beyond, moreover, were other great
foundations, bearing aloft still other groups of mounds, their declivities
thickly overgrown, but their summits betokened by the bare branches
of gumbo limbos, whence had come, no doubt, the lone-sounding songs
of the grosbeaks. They stood, these other foundations, like the sundered ramparts of some vast and ruined fortress along one side and across
the farther end of a deep open space or quadrangular court more than
an acre in extent, level and as closely covered with mangroves and

other tidal growths at the bottom as were the outer swamps. It was apparent that this had actually been a central court of some kind, had probably been formed as an open lagoon by the gradual upbuilding on attol-like reefs or shoals around deeper water, of these foundations or ramparts as I have called them, from even below tide level to their present imposing height. At any rate they were divided from one another by deep narrow gaps that appeared as though left open between them to serve as channels, and that still, although filled now with peaty deposits and rank vegetation, communicated with the outer swamps, and, in some cases, extended, between parallel banks of shell like those already described, quite through the surrounding enclosures or lesser outer courts, to what had evidently been, ere the universal sand shoals had formed and mangrove swamps had grown, the open sea.

The elevation I had ascended, stood at the northern end and formed one corner of this great inner court, the slope to which from the base of the mounds was unbroken by terraces, and sheer. But like the steepest ascents outside, it was composed of large weather-darkened conchshells and was comparatively bare of vegetation. Directly down the middle of this wide incline led, from between the two first mounds, a broad sunken pathway, very deep here near the summit, as was the opposite and similarly graded way I had in part followed up, but gradually diminishing in depth as it approached the bottom, in such manner as to render much gentler the descent to the edge of the swamp. Here numerous pierced busycon shells lay strewn about and others could be seen protruding from the marginal muck. A glance sufficed to show that they had all been designed for tool heads, hafted similarly, but used for quite various purposes. The long columnellæ of some were battered as if they had once been employed as hammers or picks, while others were sharpened to chisel or gouge-like points and edges. Here, too, sherds of pottery were much more abundant than even on the upper terraces. This struck me as especially significant, and I ventured forth a little way over the yielding quagmire and dug between the sprawling mangrove fingers as deeply as I could with only a stick, into the water-soaked muck. Similarly worked shells and sherds of pottery, intermingled with charcoal and bones, were thus revealed. These were surprisingly fresh, not as though washed into the place from above, but as though they had fallen and lodged where I found them, and had been covered with water ever since.

I suddenly realized that the place, although a central rather than a marginal court or filled-up bayou, was nevertheless similar in general character to the one Col. Durnford had described, and that thus soon my conclusions relative to the typical nature of the Collier deposit, were, in a measure, borne out. Here at least had been a water-court, around the margins of which, it would seem, places of abode whence these remains had been derived—houses rather than landings—had clustered, ere it became choked with *débris* and vegetal growth ; or else it was a veritable haven of ancient wharves and pile-dwellings, safe alike from tidal wave and hurricane within these gigantic ramparts of shell, where, through the channel gateways to the sea, canoes might readily come and go.

It occurred to me, as I made my way through one of these now filled-up channels, that the enclosures they passed were probably other courts —marginal, but artificial bayous, some of them no doubt like the one at Key Marco—and that perhaps the largest of them had not only been in-habited also, but that some were representative of incipient stages in the formation of platforms or terraces, and within these, as the key was thus extended, of other such inner courts as the one I have here described. It seemed reasonable to expect that the islets visible in numbers farther on, which my skipper described as almost exactly like this, would really prove to be not only shell keys, that is, of artificial origin, but also, that in them I would find the essential structural features of this one, as such, repeated.

Possessed by this idea, I became doubly anxious to proceed with the explorations, and forthwith returned to the boat and sailed down to a point about midway between the northern and southern ends of Pine Island, which lay some two and a half miles off to the eastward. There stood, near where we anchored, upon rough and barnacle-encrusted stilts or piles, two dilapidated platforms, placed end to end, but at an angle to one another. Upon these were perched a couple of old and weather-beaten huts which had been formerly used, I was told, as fishermen's stations.

As evening fell and the tide went down, there appeared with startling suddenness, black, in the foam of the receding waters,—much as in the illustration on Plate XXVI,—the scattered crags of two or three series of parallel and concentric oyster reefs or bars. Some of them reached directly toward us from close to the old fishing stations, while others extended off to the right, semi-circularly around us, in a long succession of level, broken masses, thus enclosing quite half an acre of deeper water, at the entrance of which we lay. It was in the shallows, between the widest of these bars, at the corner or blunt angle formed by the two main lines of the reefs, that the platforms stood. Hither now flocked hundreds of cormorants and pelicans, fol-lowed by a few cranes and curlews and by many gulls—these continu-ally on the wing. But the cormorants and pelicans settled on the plat-forms and along the uniform inner edges of the reefs in close ranks. They seemed to have come hither from the neighboring bird-keys or man-grove rookeries,—where they nested in common by thousands,—simply to rest and dress their plumage ; until, out in the channel appeared, swiftly rushing in toward the shoals, an enormous school of fish, fleeing noisily before several puffing porpoises and two or three monster sharks, whose sharp dorsal fins cut the water swiftly hither and thither in the wake of their affrighted prey. Then of a sudden the cormorants and many of the pelicans took wing, joined forces behind the on-coming fugitive hosts of the sea, and diving down in a great semi-circle, beat the waves with their wings as though in play, until, as they closed in rapidly toward the reefs, the sound made by them and the now wildly leaping fish was as that of an approaching storm. Thus thousands of the smaller fish were driven in beyond reach of the sharks and porpoises over the shoals and into the bayous formed by the succession of reefs, and there cormorants and pelicans alike made short work of securing their evening meals. The cormorants flew off singly or in swift irregular companies, but the pelicans marched more deliberately away, in orderly and single aëreal files, so to say, behind heavy-winged, gray-headed old leaders, evenly, just over the line of the waves, to their tree-built island homes.

I have dwelt on this singular behavior of the birds because, in connection with the observations of the day, and with the picture formed by the concentric reefs, the lagoon they encircled, the old half-ruined pile-houses standing above them out there in the midst of the waters, and the distant dark-green islands—which I now knew had been the homes of sea-dwelling men centuries before—disappearing beyond in the dusk, it all suggested to me in a vivid and impressive manner how the ancient builders of the key I had only this afternoon reconnoitred had probably begun their citadel of the sea and why there, so far away from the shore, they had elected to make so laboriously their homes ; why they had from the beginning kept free within their reef-raised sea-walls of shell, the central half-natural lagoons or lake-courts, where the first few of their stilted houses had doubtless been planted, and why ever, as their hand-made island extended, they had kept it surrounded with the many channeled enclosures. The key had been, so to say, the rookery, the channels and lesser enclosures the fish-drives and fish-pools of these human pelicans ! Like the pelicans, like even the modern fishermen, they had at first merely resorted to low outlying reefs in these shallow seas as fishing grounds, but ere long had built stations there, little shelters, probably, on narrow platforms held up by clumsy piles, but similar somewhat to the huts that stood here before me. The shells of the mollusks they had gathered for food had naturally been cast down beside these lengthy platforms, until they formed long ridges that broke the force of the waves when storms swept by. Thus, I fancied, these first builders of the keys had been taught how to construct with special purpose sea-walls of gathered shells, how to extend the arms of the reefs, and to make other and better bayous or fish-pounds within them by forming successive enclosures, ever keeping free channels throughout for the driving in of the fish and the passage of their canoes. And when the innermost of the enclosures became choked by drift and other *débris* they had filled them with shell stuff and mud from the surrounding sea, and so of some had made drainage-basins to catch rain for drinking water, and of others, in time, little garden plats or fields.

Thus it was that the erstwhile stations had become better and better fitted as places of longer abode ; and yet others of the enclosures or courts farthest in had become filled, and were in turn wrought into basins and gardens to replace the first that had been made ; for these were now covered over and piled higher to form wide benches whereupon the long mounds or foundations might be erected. Finally, aloft on these greater elevations strong citadels of refuge alike from foe and hurricane; storehouses, dwellings of chiefs or leaders, and assembly-places and temples had been builded, when at last these old people of the sea came to abide there continually. This to me appeared to have been the history in brief of the first development of such a phase of life as the ancient key I had examined that afternoon still plainly represented ; nor did I find reason later to greatly modify these views. On the contrary, of the many other shell keys that I examined during the following few days, all still further illustrated, and some seemed strikingly to confirm, even the most fanciful of these visions.

This was especially true of three keys which I explored the next day. The first was known as Josselyn's Key. It had been cleared and cultivated as a fruit and vegetable garden many years before, but was now abandoned and desolate and again overrun by brambles and weeds and vines, with some few massive gumbo limbos and rubber trees standing on its heights. The feature of special interest in this key was its central court, which, while comparatively small—less than half an acre in extent—was remarkably regular. Five very high and steep, moundcapped elevations, sharply divided by deep, straight channels, that led forth from the court divergingly toward the sea, formed its western side and southern end, while its opposite side and end were formed by two extensive platforms, also exceedingly steep within, and nearly as high as the elevations, and divided from these and from each other by straight canals that led forth in northwardly directions, far out through the mangrove-covered enclosures down toward which the platforms were terraced.

The court was very deep and so regular that it resembled the cellar of an enormous elongated square house. It was marshy and overgrown by cane-brakes, tall grasses, and green-barked willows. Near the mouth of the principal canal, leading forth from the southeastern corner of this court, and still invaded, as were two or three others of the canals, by high-tide water, my skipper and I dug a deep square hole. The excavation rapidly filled with water ; not, however, before we had found in the yielding muck a shapely plummet or pendant of coral-stone and two others of shell, many sherds of pottery, worked bones, charcoal, and, more significant than all, a pierced conch-shell, still containing a portion of its rotten wooden handle. Again here, the relics were more abundant than on the heights above, and the structural nature of the entire key was abundantly evident.

From this place it was somewhat more than a mile, still east-southeastwardly, to the second islet, which was known as Demorey's Key. It also had been cleared to a limited extent, by the man whose name it bore, but, like the first, had long been abandoned and was even more overgrown by vine-smothered trees and brambles—among them many pitiful limes and a few pomegranates run wild, but still faithfully bearing fruit—so that here, too, the knife was constantly requisite.

It was in some respects the most remarkable key encountered during the entire reconnaissance. Its elevations formed—as may be seen by reference to plan and elevation on Plate XXVIII,—an elongated curve five hundred yards in length, the northward extension of which was nearly straight, the southward extension bending around like a hook to the southeast and east, and embracing within its ample circuit a wide swamp thickly overgrown with high mangroves, which also narrowly fringed the outer shore, so that the whole key, when seen from the water, presented the appearance of a trim round or oval, and thickly wooded island The lower end or point of this key consisted of an imposingly massive and symmetrical sea wall, of conch-shells chiefly, ten or twelve feet high, and as level and broad on top as a turnpike. This wall had evidently once encircled the entire lower bend of the key, but was now merged in the second and third of a series of broad, comparatively level terraces, that rose one above the other within it, from a little terminal muck-court, westwardly to the central and widest, although not highest, elevation of the key, at the commencement of its northward extension. Occupying a point midway along the inner curve of this elevation, that is, directly up from the mangrove swamp it encircled on the one hand, and from the terraces outside on the other, stood a lofty group of five elongated mounds. These mounds were divided from the embracing terraces by a long, deep, and very regularly graded way, which led, in straight sections corresponding to the inner margins of the first three successive terraces, up from a canal formed by shell banks or ridges in the swamp, to the highest of the terraces—the one forming the wide central elevation. Another and much steeper and shorter graded way led up from yet another parallel canal farther within the swamp, to between the two highest mounds, down from them again, and joined this longer graded way near the point of its ascent to the high central terrace. This foundation, for it proved to be such, arose very steeply from the here sharply curved edge of the mangrove swamp, to an almost uniform height of about twenty-three feet ; was from twelve to fourteen yards wide, and thence sloped more gently toward the outer or western shores. The northern extension of the key was occupied by two or three elevated and comparatively inconsiderable mounds, beyond which it was terraced off toward the extreme point, as was the lower point—though less regularly—to a short, similar sea-wall extension eastwardly, that partly enclosed, not a muck-court, but a low, bordered garden-plat, containing two or three round sinks or basins.

The most remarkable feature of this key was a flat, elongated bench, or truncated pyramid, that crowned the middle elevation. I discovered this merely by accident. In order to gain a general idea of the key, which was almost as much overgrown with luxuriant and forbidding vegetation as had been the wilder key first explored, I climbed high up among the skinny and crooked limbs of a gigantic gumbo limbo that grew directly from the inner edge of this elevation. Luckily, great festoons of tough vines clung to the lower limbs of this tree, for in shifting my position I slipped and fell, and was caught by these vines, to the salvation of my bones probably, since by the force of the fall some of the vines were torn away, revealing the inner side of this platform and the fact that it was almost vertically faced up with conch-shells; their larger, truncated and spiral ends, laid outward and in courses so regular, that the effect was as of a mural mosaic of volutes. I hastily tore away more of the vines, and found that this faced-up edge of the platform extended many feet in either direction from the old gumbo limbo. I may say here, that on occasion of two later visits I cleared the façade of this primitive example of shell architecture still more; was enabled, indeed, when I last visited the place—since I was then accompanied by a considerable force of workmen—to entirely expose its inner side and its southern end. Thus was revealed—even more completely than is shown in Plate XXIX,—a parallelogrammic and level platform, some three and a half feet high and twelve yards in width, by nearly thrice as many in length. It was approached from the inner side by a graded way that led obliquely along the curved ascent up from the mangrove swamp, to a little step-like, subsidiary platform half as high and some twelve feet square, which joined it at right angles, just beyond the point shown at the extreme right of the picture here given. The top of this lesser step, and the approaches to either side of it, were paved with very large, uniform-sized clam-shells, laid convex sides upward, and as closely and regularly as tiles. The lower or southern end of the main platform was rounded at the corners, and rounded also on either side of the sunken ascent midway, in which the longer of the graded ways I have described terminated. Contemplating the regularity of this work, its central position, and its evident importance as indicated by the several graded ways leading to it from distant points, I could not doubt that it had formed the foundation of an imposing temple-structure, and this idea was further carried out by the presence at its northern end of two small, but quite prominent altar-like mounds.

Descending from the end of the platform down along the main graded way—the one which divided the terraces from the central group of high mounds—I found that at more than one point, the sides of this deep, regular path, had also been faced up with conch-shells, though none of the courses were now, to any extent, in place.

At the foot of the inner and parallel sided, sunken or graded way—the one descending from between two of the great central mounds—I caused an excavation to be made between the two straight banks or ridges of shell that extended thence far out into the mangrove swamp, in order to ascertain whether this supposed canal had really been such; that is,

an open way or channel to the sea for canoes. It became evident that
it had been this, for we were able to excavate through vegetal muck
and other accumulated *débris* to a depth of more than four feet, although
much inconvenienced by inflowing water. I thus found that the shell-
banks had not only been built up with a considerable degree of regularity, but that, well defined as these ridges were, the portions of them visible above the muck were merely their crests. The excavation was made
near what may thus be regarded as having formed the original landing,
and in it we found a considerable number of quite well-preserved relics,
similar to those I had found in the court on Josselyn's key. Another
excavation made near the termination of the two embankments, however, revealed fewer artificial remains, other than blackened and water-
worn sherds of pottery. But I found that here also, the artificial banks
or walls, so to call them, had been built up with equal regularity, almost
vertically, from a depth of between four and five feet. In extending
this excavation, an interesting feature of the original foundations of
these outworks was revealed. It consisted of a kind of shell breccia
formed of the first layers of shells that had been placed there—that
were composed of conchs, some of which had been driven or wedged,
smaller ends first, into the original reef or bar, and had apparently been
further solidified by a filling or packing of tough clay-like marl, now
so indurated that shell, sherds of pottery, and here and there bits of bone
and charcoal formed, with it, a solid mass well progressed toward fossili-
zation. Indeed, when large fragments of this time-hardened cement were
pried up and broken open, the shell, sherds of pottery and bones contained in them appeared already like fossils. I found by making yet other
excavations in the contiguous and almost untraceable courts or enclosures, that they, too, had been built up from an equal depth, as though to
serve rather as fish-pounds than as breakwaters or as courts to the quays
and houses, for the crests of these enclosures so slightly protruded above
the surface of the muck and weedy carpeting of the mangrove swamp in
which they occurred, that I had at first quite failed to observe them. Thus
it appeared that this half-enclosed swamp, no less than the swamps surrounding the first key I had examined, contained similar sorts of enclosures, only these had been lower originally, or else had since been more
filled in with muck, vegetal growth and tide-wash. The low-bordered
terrace or garden plot, the margin of which faced this swamp within
the northern end of the key, was wide and comparatively level, except
that in one or two places toward the slopes of the terraces next above it,
there occurred in it the circular holes I have mentioned as basins, one
of which looked almost like a well. The like of these I later encountered
on many others of the keys, and they seemed to be catch-basins for rain or
places for water storage, artificial çenotes, as it were, like the spring-holes
or sink-holes on the mainland and in Yucatan. Moreover, the surrounding plot, like the terraces at the lower end of the key, and like those I
had found on the first island I had explored, was scantily supplied with

black soil intermixed with the shells, and here I observed that although relics of other sorts were comparatively rare, fish-bones formed a considerable proportion of this soil, as though fish or the refuse of fish had been used here for fertilizing purposes. All these observations, taken in connection with the highly finished condition of the crowning platform, of the beautifully paved approaches to it, of the walls or sides of the long-graded path, and of the terminal sea-walls themselves, clearly demonstrated the artificial origin of not only such portions of the key as stood above low-tide level, but also, the highly structural character of the whole work—as I now considered it to be,—of the island in its entirety.

Visible from Demorey's key, a mile and a half or two miles away in a northeasterly direction, stood a promontory, island-like in appearance, on account of its relative boldness. Learning from my sailor that it was really on Pine Island, and that there also were extensive shell accumulations, and that in the depths of the pine lands beyond were other and larger mounds of quite different character, I paid a hasty visit to the place.

It was known as Battey's Landing, although the "landing" had to be approached by wading a long way, for the tide was low. And as we neared it we were greeted by the barking of a small colony of hounds and other dogs. A solitary man appeared, who occupied one of two small huts that stood some way up from the shore. His name was Kirk, and he was most hospitable and helpful to me. He and his partner, Captain Rhodes, worked the place as a vegetable farm, and were now again most profitably cultivating its ancient gardens. However, I soon saw that it had once been like the outer islets—an artificial key—but so much closer in-shore, even originally, that it had become connected with the main part of Pine Island by extensive sand flats, still so low as to be washed by high tides. The foundations, mounds, courts, graded ways and canals here were greater, and some of them even more regular, than any I had yet seen. On the hither or seaward side many enclosures, overgrown of course by mangroves, flanked wide benches or garden platforms, through or over which led paths, mostly obliterated by cultivation now. The same sorts of channel-ways as occurred on the outer keys led up to the same sorts of terraces and great foundations, with their coronets of gigantic mounds. The inner or central courts were enormous. Nearly level with the swamps on the one hand, and with the sand flats on the other, these muck-beds were sufficiently extensive to serve (having been cleared and drained as far as possible) as rich and ample gardens ; and they were framed in, so to say, by quadrangles formed by great shell structures which, foundation terraces, summit-mounds and all, towered above them to a height of more than sixty feet.

There were no fewer than nine of these greater foundations, and within or among them no fewer than five large, more or less rectangular courts ; and, beyond all, to the southward, was a long series of lesser benches, courts and enclosures, merging off into scarce visible fragments in the white, bare stretches of sand flats. Suffice it, if I say, that this settlement had an average width of a quarter of a mile, and extended along the shore of Pine Island—that is from north to south—more than three-quarters of a mile ; that its high-built portions alone, including of course, the five water courts, covered an area of not less than seventy-five or eighty acres. The inner courts were all, except one, furnished with outlets that had originally opened through short canals into the strait that had separated the key from the main island. The single exception referred to was notable. The midmost of these inner courts, which was too low to be made use of as a garden, and was therefore still overgrown with enormous mangrove, button-wood and other trees, was, or had been, connected with the sea by a canal that led into it between two long, very high shell elevations, which flanked it on either side of the western end. From the opposite end of the court another canal led directly eastward into the pine lands. Not to pause with a further account of this greatest, except one, of all the monuments of the ancient key builders on the Florida coast, save to say that in the court of the canals I found the finest and best preserved relics I had yet discovered. I will only describe this landward canal and the gigantic mounds and other inland works to which it led. It extended in a straight line almost due eastwardly across the sand flats, that were, at this point, very narrow, and heavily overgrown with canebrakes and high grasses ; while beyond, palmettos and yuccas covered the entire plain far into the pine-lands. It was uniformly about thirty feet wide, and though of course now much filled, especially between the shell-made levees that crossed the flats, it still maintained an even depth of between five and six feet. A few yards beyond where it entered the higher level of the pine lands, there was a little outlet from its southern side, which led straight to what had been an enormous artificial pond or oval lake, that was still so boggy I could not traverse it. From the opposite end of this lake, in turn, led for nearly a quarter of a mile further, in a generally southeastern direction, but not in a straight line, another and lesser canal. It terminated in another artificial lake, that extended east and west, and in the middle of this stood, crosswise, a gigantic and shapely mound. This mound was oval in outline, fifty-eight feet high, some three hundred and seventy-five feet in length and a little more than one hundred and fifty feet in the width at its base. A graded way wound around it spirally from the southern base to the summit, which was comparatively narrow, but long and level like the tops of the shell mounds on the keys. Ascending this mound, I found that it had been built up of sand and thin strata of sea-shells alternately, and that to the presence of these strata of shells had been due, probably, the remarkable preservation of its form. Potsherds of fine quality, chalky remains of human bones, broken shell ladles—their bottoms significantly punctured—all demontrated the fact that this mound, which obviously had been used as the foundation of a temple structure, had also served as a place of burial.

Due northeast from it, half a mile farther in, might be seen another and even larger mound, double, not single-crested, like this. The great canal, a branch of which opened into the encircling lake of this mound also, led on directly past it, and could be plainly traced, even from this distance, through the palmetto-covered plain beyond. Again, in a southwest direction, not quite so far away, I could discern among the scattered pines a hummock, comparatively low and small, but regular and overgrown thickly with palmettos and brambles. It, too, proved to be a mound, mostly of shell, but probably built for burial purposes, yet furnished like these two larger ones, with a contiguous lake or pond hole, from which also led a slight canal to the near-by sand flats. Returning to the greater canal and following it out to the point of its connection with the lake of the double mound, I found that the eastern end of this lake was large, rather square than round, and that it formed really a water-court fronting the mound and more or less surrounded originally with embankments—of sand chiefly—but like the characteristic shell embankments of the keys in form, as if, indeed, made purposely to resemble them. From this excavated lake-court, a graded way had also once led up the eastern side of the double mound, its terminus forming, in fact, the saddle between its two summits—that reached an altitude of more than sixty-three feet. In all these regards it exactly resembled one of the great shell foundations—crowning mounds and all—of the outer keys, and I could not but be impressed with the apparent significance of this, especially as I found by slight excavation that the mound had been composed, like the other, of shell strata in part, and that it was erected veritably as a foundation, since there was no evidence that it had been used to any great extent as a burial place. Moreover, the great canal, turning a little to the southeast, led on again in a straight line into the interior. I followed it for more than a mile, and, although it lessened in width, it was distinctly traceable still beyond, and I was told that it extended quite across the island to similar works and shell elevations on the other side. I later learned that the canal and mounds on Naples Island were not unlike these, although smaller, and that equally gigantic works occurred far up the great rivers of the coast, as far up the Caloosahatchee, for instance, as Lake Okeechobee and the Everglades. Everywhere, too, these inland works resembled, with their surroundings—embankments, court or bayou-like lakes, canals, graded ways, etc —the works of the keys. And I have been led to infer that they actually represent the first stage of a later and inland phase of key-dweller modes of building, and furnish a hint that, perhaps not only other inland mounds of Florida, but also the great and regular mounds and other earth-works occurring in the lowlands of our Southern and Middle Western States, and celebrated as the remains of the so-called mound-builders, may likewise also be traced, if not to this beginning, at least to a similar beginning in some seashore and marshland environment. I shall therefore recur to the subject specifically in later paragraphs.

Immediately after completing this examination of what I regarded as one of the most recent and highly developed works of the ancient key-builders, I proceeded down the Sound to St. James City, at the southern end of Pine Island. Fortunately I bore friendly letters of introduction from Colonel J. M. Kreamer, of Philadelphia, to Captain E. White-side, the principal resident of the little city. He welcomed me most hospitably, and extended to me whatever help it was possible for him to give.

Curiously enough, the three or four places next examined by me after my arrival at St. James City, were as illustrative of the *beginnings* of the key-dweller modes of life as had been the remains I had last explored, of their later development.

At the extreme southeastern point of Pine Island occurred the first of these. It consisted chiefly of a single long and, throughout the lower portions of its course, double-crested shell embankment, from four to nine feet high. I was at once struck by the fact that this great shell ridge, which was more than thirty-five hundred feet in length, was made up in parts, or comparatively short, straight sections, placed end to end, so that its general contour was more or less polygonal, for it partially encircled a wide mangrove swamp on its inner or landward side, within which could be faintly seen here and there low shell-bank enclosures such as I have so frequently described heretofore. I have said that this shell ridge was in some places double, or rather double-crested. These double or parallel crests along its summit were here and there still so sharp that they distinctly appeared to have been formed by deposition from above. This suggested to me that in the beginning, a series of straight, narrow platforms or scaffolds had been erected end to end over the curved outlying reef here, and that shells—perhaps mere refuse at first, precisely as I had imagined when looking at the old Fishing Station, above—had been cast down along either side of these platforms until a nucleus of the ridge was thus formed. At two points, however, the works had been widened and more regularly built up, as though at these points the beginnings of characteristic terraces and of at least one foundation had been made. But nowhere else was there evidence that this ancient structure had progressed much beyond its earliest, its fishing-station-stage of construction. It appeared to me that ere it had been possible for the ancient builders to carry their work here further towards making a permanent home, some hurricane or great tidal wave had overwhelmed them, or had so far destroyed their station or incipient settlement as to render its further completion undesirable or impossible; and that thus we had preserved to us in this place an evidence of their modes of beginning such stations or settlements. Again, at the opposite or southwestern point or corner of Pine Island had stood another great shell ridge, higher, wider, generally curved also, and a little further progressed towards formation as a permanent settlement; for at its upper end there remained evidence that it

had possessed narrow terraces and two or three considerable foundations. The greater portion of this work, however, had been removed
by Captain Whiteside—at a cost of more than ten thousand dollars—for
use in the construction of a boulevard around the end of the island and
of crossroads through the marshy space it enclosed. Miles of shell-
road—the most beautiful in southwestern Florida—had thus been made,
yet still the shell material of this one old-time beginning merely, of a
key, had not thereby been wholly exhausted. Few relics, other than a
couple of skeletons and numerous shreds of pottery and fragments of
broken shell tools, had been encountered during the demolition of the
structure ; yet it was plain that it had been built on low encircling
reefs up from the very level of the water as had all the others.

Another work, quite similar to this, but still undisturbed, was found
by me straight across Carlos Bay,—as the body of water to the south and
west of Pine Island and at the mouth of the Caloosahatchee river was
called—on one of the inner marginal reefs of Sanybel Island, the lower
end of which formed here a great loop around the bay and entrance referred to. At this point the ancient key-builders had succeeded in progressing a stage or two further in the construction of one of their settlements
ere they had been, evidently in like manner as at the other places, overwhelmed by some catastrophe. Such portions of the work as were
left—for some part of it had been destroyed and washed away by successive storms—formed more of an enclosure of mangrove swamp than
did either of those last described. It had been considerably widened
and built up, at its middle, and again towards its western end. Well-
defined canals led in from among shell-bank enclosures within the mangrove swamp to both of these built-up points, the westernmost terminating in a diminutive inner court. At both points, too, the foundations of
mound-terraces had been begun. Digging in towards the middle of one
of these incipient terraces from the outer shore line, I encountered not
only numerous relics, but also large, flat fragments of breccia-like
cement. Further up, on the more level portion of this terrace, I found
that the cement was continuous over a considerable space, but that the
bed thus formed abruptly ended along a line parallel with the western
edge or end of the elevation. At almost regular intervals along this
line occurred holes in the compact substratum of shell, formed by the
decaying of stout posts that had been set therein—as was shown by lin-
gering traces of rotten wood that occurred in each. Thus it appeared
that this flat bed of cement had once formed a thin vertical wall, or
rather the plastering of a timber-supported wall, probably the end of
some large building which had crowned the terrace, and that had fallen
in under the stress of some storm or as a result of other accident.

To ascertain whether the works here were, like the outworks of
Demorey's key, originally founded upon a shallow or submerged reef,
I caused a trench several feet long to be excavated down to between
eighteen inches and two feet below mean tide-level. I thus ascertained

that here, as on Demorey's key, the whole structure had, indeed, been built up on a shoal or reef; a solid foundation of very large conch-shells having first been driven into the original reef, but not apparently here reinforced with clay-marl; smaller shells of many kinds having then, in turn, been piled on this, and fhat finally—as shown by the talus of uniform-sized conchs around the base of the terrace—the outer and inner faces of the whole elevation had been covered over or faced up with courses of these beautiful shells. The examination of the mere beginning of a station or a settlement at the southern end of Pine Island, then of this further advanced remnant of ancient work, demonstrated to me the correctness of the inference I ventured, prematurely perhaps, to mention in an earlier portion of this paper. The finding here, also, of what was almost unmistakably the outer coating or plastering of a temple or some other kind of large building upon one of the flat terraces or mounds, such as I have so often described as found on the upper keys in more perfected condition, seemed also to indicate as unmistakably that these mounds, wherever found, had been designed as the foundations of such buildings of a more or less permanent and probably public or tribal character.

A long, very low sand-spit, comparatively narrow, and covered with mangroves, extended in a direction parallel with the curved inner shores of Sanybel Island, from very near the end of this ancient settlement to almost the end of the island itself. This low bar, joined by another that put out from the oppositely curved shore of the island, enclosed a round body of water known as Ellis' Bay. I heard that Captain Ellis, the long-time resident of the place, had found near his quaint palmetto huts on its southern shore, a few days previously, some human bones. I visited his place. I would fain describe it in all its picturesqueness,— the thatched houses irregularly set on the low flat stretch of sand, amid clumps of native palmettos and luxuriant groves of lime, orange, and other tropical fruit trees ; but can only pause to make due acknowledgment of his whole-souled courtesy and helpfulness during the prosecution of my hasty excavations there. Behind his little assemblage of huts, the land rose gradually to a considerable height, consisting almost wholly of sea sand, that had been drifted over from the opposite beaches of the gulf. This sand drift had in the course of centuries quite buried a low but extensive ancient shell settlement. A drainage canal, that had recently been dug by settlers living farther up the island, revealed to me the previously unsuspected presence of this settlement, and the fact that it, like all the others I have described, had been built up originally from reefs or shoals. From it, a sort of causeway of conch-shells had once led out towards a nearly round, enclosed space, closer to the present shore, and off to the westward side of Ellis' place. This enclosure was now, of course, filled with boggy muck and overgrown ; but it surrounded a somewhat extensive, low mound, composed in part of shells and in part of black soil. The mound (or hammock, as such mounds in lowlands are universally called in that section of the country) was under cultivation as a vegetable and fruit garden ; and it was in the attempt to remove from it the roots of a large stump, that Captain Ellis had made the find of human bones I had heard of. In excavating near by, I discovered that the whole heap was permeated, so to say, with broken human remains ; large bones and small, many of which had been split or shattered, mingled with skulls, some few fortunately still entire, although very fragile. I succeeded in securing eleven of these skulls before leaving. Few relics of any other sort, save now and then punctured shell ladles, were encountered ; but it was perfectly obvious that the place had been a true bone-heap, established on a slight artificial elevation in the midst of an ancient enclosed pond or water court, and it was also evident that the human remains therein deposited, had been dismembered before burial, for ceremonial purposes probably—had been even broken up in some cases. I later learned that this place was typical of the ossuaries or lake-enclosed cemeteries almost invariably found on the ancient keys, and came to look upon these curious little mortuary lakes or water courts, with their overfilled central islets, as having been thus framed and fashioned to be, as it were, miniature Keys or Shell Settlements of the Dead Key Dwellers buried therein.

I believe I have now described sufficiently typical examples of the ancient artificial shell islands—or, as I like better to call them, "Keys"— of these inland seas of the southwestern coast of Florida.

Ere passing on to the scene of our long continued and more thorough examination of one of the most ancient and characteristic of these, however, it may be well for me to mention that there were, in Charlotte Harbor, Pine Island Sound, Caloosa Entrance and Matlatcha Bay alone, more than seventy-five of them. Forty of this number were gigantic, the rest were representative of various stages in the construction of such villages of the reefs. No doubt a more searching exploration of these waters, and of the wide and forbidding mangrove swamps on contiguous shores of Sanybel, and of others of the outer islands, and of Pine Island, as well as of the mainland itself, would reveal many others ; but the amount of work represented even by the number I have already named is so enormous and astounding, that it cannot be realized or appreciated by means of mere spoken description or statement.

Beyond the incurving lower point of Sanybel Island, it was necessary to make the rest of my journey through the open Gulf ; not that another series of narrower inland seas did not lie within similar narrow, sandy islands, but because I could not pause to examine their islet-studded reaches. I stopped at only two places on my way to Key Marco, which was still between forty and forty-five miles further to the southward. One was at Mound Key or Johnson's Key, as it was variously called. I make mention of my visit to the place principally because of its great extent. It consisted of a long series of enormous elevations crowned by imposing mounds that reached an average altitude of over sixty feet. They were interspersed with deep inner courts, and widely surrounded with enclosures that were threaded by broad, far-reaching canals, so that this one key included an area of quite two hundred acres, within which area may be reckoned only such surface as had been actually reclaimed by the ancient key builders from this inland or shore-land sea. I was told by Mrs. Johnson, wife of the owner of the place, to whom good Mrs. Ellis had kindly given me a characteristic letter of introduction, that burial mounds, not unlike the one on the Ellis place, but larger, occurred in the depths of the wide mangrove swamps that lay below towards the mainland, and that here on the heights, many Spanish relics had been found—Venetian beads, scraps of sheet copper, small ornaments of gold and silver, and a copper-gilt locket. She showed me this. It contained a faded portrait, and a still more faded letter, written on yellow parchment, apparently from some Spanish Grandee of about two hundred years ago to a resident colonist of that time.

Whether these relics indicated that here the ancient key dwellers or their mixed descendants had lingered on into early historic times, and that the Mission that these things betokened, had been established among them, or among alien successors, could not, of course, be determined ; but around the lower courts, and on the old garden terraces, I found abundant specimens of shell and coarse pottery, characteristic of the key dwellers proper who had anciently built this island, and since returning I have carefully examined an interesting series of both kinds of relics gathered here by your fellow-member, Mr. Joseph Wilcox, which offer even better evidence of this, and are now I am happy to say preserved in the University museum.

I made only a brief stop at Naples City. Captain Large of that place, to whom I bore a letter of introduction, received me most courteously, and showed me, nearby, the mouth of the ancient canal, of which I had already heard from Col. Durnford. Except that it once opened in directly from the Gulf and had evidently been designed as a canoe pass across the island, it was in many respects like the one I had examined on Pine Island, although deeper and at the same time narrower. I was told by Captain Large that like mounds, too, occurred near its outlet on the farther side, and that it terminated in front of some ancient shell works out in the inner bay beyond, similar, I judged, to those at Battey's Landing.

From Naples City the sail to Marco was short ; for squalls were rising out over the Gulf, making its opalescent waters tumultuous and magnificent, but to my sailors, terrible, driving us now and anon furiously fast through the rising billows, what though our sails were reefed low. Big Marco Pass opened tortuously between two islands of sand ; the northern one narrow, long and straight, backed by mangrove swamps ; the southern one broad, generally flat but undulating, and covered with tall, lank grasses, scattered, scrubby trees, and stately palmettos. The mangrove swamps, sundered by numerous inlets on the one side, this wide, straight-edged sandy island on the other, bordered the inlet that led straight eastward a mile or more to the majestic cocoanut grove that fronted Collier's Bay and Key Marco. I will not describe the key greatly in detail, for an admirable contour map of it, made with great care by Mr. Wells M. Sawyer, artist of the expedition I later conducted to the place, is furnished herewith. The key, like Battey's Landing, like Johnson's key, and many other places of the kind, was now more or less connected with contiguous land; yet obviously, when built and occupied, it had stood out in the open waters. It was not even yet joined to Caximbas Island, at the northwestern angle of which it stood, save by a wide and long mangrove swamp that was still washed daily by high tide. As may be seen by the plan,—on Plate XXX,— a number of long, straight and narrow canals, terminating in little court-like landings and short graded ways, stretched in from the western side, the lower end of which was enclosed and extended by a massive, level-topped sea-wall, now used as a wagon road, reaching nearly a quarter of a mile into the mangrove swamps, and indicating that when it was built, this had been the stormward side, which it had therefore been necessary to protect. There were other indications that the extensive sand bank or island which now fronted the key across Collier's Bay on this gulf-ward side, as well as the long reaches of mangrove swamp to the southward, had all been formed, in the main, since the date of its occupancy. This was notably the case with many other keys in the neighborhood of Key Marco, which keys formed, with the intermediate mangrove islets,—mere seg-regated sections of swamp they appeared, scarcely rising above the tide level,—the northernmost of the great archipelago of the Ten Thousand Islands. Explorations among these border islands, within a radius of from fifteen to twenty miles around Key Marco, demonstrated the fact that on an average about one in every five of them was an ancient shell settlement or key proper like Marco and the others already described, and that the low-lying intermediate islets had mostly been formed on shoals caused by drift, around and between these obstructions built by man, since the time of their occupation. Again, around each one of these more southerly shell keys or settlements, the fringe of the mangrove swamps was far deeper, or wider, than around the more northerly keys, indicating that a much greater time had elapsed since their abandonment; time enough for the formation of many miles of sand bank, and the growth thereon of the mangrove swamps around and between them. Marco inlet, or the eastward and southward exten-sion of Big Marco Pass, formed to the northeast and east of Key Marco a comparatively wide, deep bay. The edge of the key along this bay had evidently been worn away to some extent, so that its eastern face afforded in places sectional views of its structure that told the same story with regard to this key that my excavations had told with regard to Demorey's and the little keys in the neighborhood of St. James City;

namely, that although far more extensive and quite lofty, this, no less than they, had been built from the very sea level upward. Two or three straight, deep and regular canals led in from this side also, one in particular, directly through the loftier terraces here, to the central elevation of the place. This reached a height of only eighteen or nineteen feet, yet it was still remarkably regular, nearly parallelogrammic, flat-topped, and upon its level summit stood—in place, probably, of the ancient temple that once surmounted it (for there occurred here, as on the pyramid-platform of Demorey's key, an altar-like mound near the northern end)—the house now occupied by Captain Cuthbert, part owner, with Captain Collier, of Key Marco. A graded way descended slantingly across the lower end of this eminence, into what had first been a central court, like the one on Josselyn's key. This, however, had in course of time been filled purposely, and the canal that had led straight into it from the south had been filled in too, so as to form a prolongation of the graded way down to the edge of the great court or muck-filled bayou that was embraced within the two lateral and southern extensions of the key. In the southeastern portion of these broad flat canal-seamed extensions, might be seen still two or three remarkably regular and deep circular tanks or çenotes, as I have called them, whence straight sunken ways led up to the easternmost of the series of broad foundations and mounds that, with other filled-in garden courts between, flanked the central eminence or temple-pyramid on either side. Just inside of the sea wall that protected the southwestern edge of the key occurred the little triangular muck-court which had been dug into first by Captain Collier, Mr. Wilkins, and Colonel Durnford.

I was most courteously received by Captain Collier; both he and his neighbor, Captain Cuthbert, gave me entire freedom to explore wheresoever I would, and in whatsoever manner. As may be seen by the accompanying plan of the "Court of the Pile Dwellers," (thus I later named this place) I caused an excavation to be made to one side of and just beyond those that had been made by the gentlemen mentioned (see plan, Plate XXXI, Sections 34, 44). A single day's work in this boggy, mangrove-covered, water-soaked, muck and peat bed, revealed not only other such relics as I had found in the keys above, but a considerable number of well-preserved objects of wood, including more of the kind I had seen in Colonel Durnford's possession, and, what was especially significant, the remains of short piles, of slight timbers, of a long, beautifully finished spruce-wood spar, of charcoal, and fragments of indurated material that had once formed the heat-hardened plaster of hearths. There were also small masses of much decayed thatch, apparently for house-roofing or siding, I judged, and not a few unfinished objects, to say nothing of abundant refuse of meals. All which indicated that my inference in regard to the nature of this place as an actual site of former residence was as tenable as had been the more general conclusion that it was not a solitary example of its kind. Key Marco, water-courts, canals, elevations, central mounds, cistern holes, garden terraces and all, was, that is, but another such as were the keys further north. I scarcely paused in this preliminary reconnaissance to do more than determine this most significant point, but prosecuted the excavation only during a portion of the following day, then packed up my already considerable collection, and securing permission from Captain Collier, to bring men and more thoroughly excavate the place another year, returned to St. James City.

There, with Captain Whiteside's ready help, I secured the services of an intelligent and interested Scotchman, Alexander Montgomery by name, and of Johnny Smith, an active and bright young pilot of the place. With them, I reëxamined and excavated to some extent, in the keys I had already seen, and in some others around Pine Island ; finding only more and more reason to regard them as of such kind as I have already described.

The rainy season had set in. The heat was excessive, although it was only early June. The mosquitoes and sand flies swarmed forth from the mangroves in such clouds that wherever we dug, except on one or two of the comparatively barren and lofty keys, it was necessary for us to build smudge-fires all around us and breathe their pungent smoke in order to be free from these irritating creatures. I mention this, not because I was forced to abandon work thereby, but since it offered one more explanation—an important one, it seemed to me—of the causes that had led to the building and occupation of these ancient keys so far out in the shallow but open waters, where, ere the mangroves grew, men were comparatively free from these pests of life in southern Florida

These additional explorations quite convinced me that in those yet unnumbered tropic islands lay a vast, comparatively new and very promising field for archæological research, and with this thought and its warrant in the way of collections, I hastened back to Philadelphia and made report to Doctor Pepper.

ORGANIZATION OF THE PEPPER-HEARST ARCHÆOLOGICAL EXPEDITION.

I am happy to say that Dr. Pepper, with the ready aid of several of his friends and associates, immediately planned to fit out under my direction, during the following winter, an expedition for the more complete exploration of this interesting region. At a meeting held soon after my return, Mr. Jacob Disston generously volunteered not only to make a contribution—as did several other Associates of the Archæological Department of the University, whom I would fain mention—but, also, to turn over for our use his schooner, the *Silver Spray*, belonging to a fleet of sponging vessels at Tarpon Springs, some twenty-five miles north of Tampa, on the west coast of Florida. Almost as speedily, too, Major J. W. Powell, Director of the Bureau of American Ethnology, provisionally granted me leave, and promise of official recognition and assistance in the conduct of this proposed expedition in the joint interest of the Bureau itself, and of the Department of Archæology of the University of Pennsylvania.

Funds were placed at my disposal by Dr. Pepper late in November, 1896, and happily I was able to secure the volunteer services of Mr. Wells M. Sawyer, to be Artist and Photographer of the expedition ; of Mr. Irving Sayford, of Harrisburg, to be its Field Secretary ; and, for a small salary, of Mr. Carl F. W. Bergmann, previously trained as a Preparator of Collections, in the United States National Museum.

The Clyde Line Steamship Company again laid us under obligation by furnishing passes for all of these gentlemen, from New York City to Jacksonville and Sanford. They left Washington on the fourth day of December. Two days later, Mrs. Cushing and I left overland, and joined them at Jacksonville. Without delay we proceeded thence via Sanford, to Tarpon Springs.

EXPLORATIONS IN THE REGION OF TARPON SPRINGS.

Unfortunately I found that the *Silver Spray* had but recently been sent away on another sponging cruise, and that I could not expect her return for some time. Anxious as I was to proceed with the exploration of the shores and keys further to the southward, nevertheless, it became necessary, in order that time be not lost, to prosecute investigations in the less novel, but still, archæologically rich fields around Tarpon Springs and in the region of the Anclote river,—upon a bayou of which this beautiful little winter resort was situated.

Since Mr. Clarence B. Moore, of this city, has for a number of years conducted, with rare skill and great success, explorations among mounds and the ancient camp sites of other more easterly portions of Florida, and since the collections he has gathered there, more or less resemble those that we were able to gather in the burial mounds and camp sites of the Tarpon Springs region, and have been admirably illustrated to the world in his various monographs, I will, in this paper, pass over the results of our explorations there very lightly.

We met helpful friends at Tarpon Springs. Messrs. Cheyney and Marvin assigned to us comfortable quarters in one of their hotel cottages and subsequently aided us in many ways ; and it was my especial good fortune to meet Mr. Leander T. Safford, adopted son of the founder of Tarpon Springs, and to be conducted by him, on the very day of our arrival, to an ancient burial mound lying at the foot of the village, on land belonging to the Safford Estates. This little mound was low and apparently unimportant, for it had been superficially honeycombed by relic hunters ; yet a few scattered fragments of bone, associated with mortuary potsherds, indicated to me not only that it had been extraordinarily rich in burials, but, also, that in its depths many of the interments still remained undisturbed. Accordingly I forthwith engaged workmen to excavate it systematically and thoroughly—a labor that occupied several weeks. During its progress, however, we encountered the remains of more than six hundred skeletons. These, with notable exceptions—probably those of chiefs and head men—had been dismembered previously to interment, but were distributed in distinct groups that I regarded as communal or totemic and phratral, and of exceeding interest; for they seemed to indicate that the burial-mound had been regarded by its builders as a tribal settlement, a sort of "Little City of their Dead," and that if so, it might be looked on as still, in a measure, representing the distribution and relations of the clans and phratries in an actual village or tribal settlement of these people.when living. Moreover, in the minor disposition of the skeletons that had not been scattered, but had been buried in packs, or else entire and extended, in sherd-lined graves or wooden cists within and around each of these groups, it seemed possible to still trace somewhat of the relative ranks of individuals in these groups, and not a few of the social customs and religious beliefs of the ancient builders. This possibility was still further borne out by the fact that with the skeletal remains were associated, in differing ways, many superb examples of pottery and sacrificial potsherds, and numerous stone, shell and bone utensils, weapons, and ornaments. That the Safford mound was typical was conclusively shown when we were permitted by Captain Hope, of Anclote, to excavate a similar, although larger and higher mound, on land of his at Finley Hammock, some nine miles to the northwestward of Tarpon Springs, and when we found there also, abundant similar interments and relics of like kinds, similarly distributed.

Of all the art remains we recovered from these two mounds, none possessed greater interest than the pottery. Considerable numbers of unusual forms were found, including terra-cotta drums, tall, very ornate cups or vases, and small flat-bottomed bowls, decorated by means of etched and carved lines, some of these carved designs being maskoidal in character, and obviously derived, as were the stamped and otherwise wrought surface designs on countless sherds in the collection, from woodenware forms and designs. By far the most interesting class of this pottery was, however, such of it as had been decorated by punctation—literally by tattooing—not merely, I judged, in imitation of tattooed totemic designs on the persons of those who had made and used it,—but in an effort to veritably transfer or reproduce these designs; so that in studying them I recognized much in regard to the totemic organization, and still more in relation to the mythic concepts of their makers. I also perceived in these significances and designs, some of which correlated perfectly with those shown on the paintings of Florida Indians given me by my lamented friend, the late Doctor G. Brown Goode, and reproduced from water colors made by the Limner of Laudonnier's Expedition to Florida more than three hundred years ago—

the first clear evidence thus far known to us, of that kind of personification-transfer by means of tattoo or paint, with which primitive artists seem ever to have sought to animate their own particular utensils—food and water vessels especially—and to thus relate them personally to themselves. And I can safely say that a prolonged study of these collections, so strikingly and unusually suggestive in this respect, would throw more light upon primitive decorations, as being in the nature of symbolic investures, not primarily of artistic and æsthetic expression, than any others yet, so far as I am aware, gathered.

There was a feature in connection with these Tarpon Springs and Anclote burial-mounds, that was more specifically significant to me. All of them were surrounded by what at first appeared to be moats. Excavation made it evident, however, that in case of at least the Safford and Hope mounds, these encircling depressions were rather the borders of artificial basins, which had been not only purposely, but also most laboriously, hollowed out, and in the midst of which, it was clear, the mounds had been built, not at once, but in stages, corresponding to successive periods of interment ; for they were distinctly stratified, and moreover the remains in the lowermost stratum occurred at a depth greater than that of the muck-filled bottoms of the moat-like depressions surrounding them. This lake-mound kind of burial seemed to indicate survival of key-dweller modes of burial—hence its specific significance to me. That is, I looked upon it as probably being a later, an inland form of bone deposition in an enclosed water-, or lake-court—here imitative, no doubt—such as I had examined at Ellis' Place on Sanybel Island. Moreover, the "Hammocks" or inland shell-heaps or camp-sites, associated with these burial-mounds of the Tarpon Springs and Anclote region likewise possessed key-dweller features ; in the earth-works, graded ways, artificial lakes or pond-holes, and canals usually contained within or around them ; as though these, in turn, were survivals of or were copied from key-dweller modes of settlement—the works of successors or descendants of the key dwellers following out here in the marshes of the mainland, their characteristic—and erstwhile necessary—modes of building and settlement in the shallow seas. From all this and from evidence of similar survival in art shown abundantly by the collections we gathered from these mounds and camp-sites of the northerly Gulf region, I believed that a bridge, alike in time and in art and cultural development, might be established between the pristine key dwellers of the South, as exemplified by their great shell structures, fish courts, mound terraces, and works in wood and shell, and the historic mound-building Indians not only of northern Florida, but also, possibly even of our nearer Southern States—as pictured by the early chroniclers—who describe them as having been settled in lowland villages clustering around mounds or pyramids of earth that were surmounted by temples and other public buildings, approached by canoe channels and graded ways, provided with fish-ponds or lakes, and with temples of the dead sequestered in nearby deep forests or swamps.

THE CRUISE TO THE TEN THOUSAND ISLANDS AND PRELIMINARY
OPERATIONS AT KEY MARCO.

The *Silver Spray* was tardy in returning, and, withal, had to be over-
hauled. Thus it was not until late in February that we were able to
fully equip her and get under way for the southern keys—explorations in
which had been from the beginning, the main object of the Expedition.
We were provided with provisions for two months, and with a working
outfit which, although the best I could purchase on the west coast of
Florida, would have proven all too inadequate but for the kindness of
friends before mentioned, and in particular, of a resident of your city
and member of your University Archæological Association, Mrs. Richard
Levis, who, with her friend, Mrs. George Inness, was passing the winter
in her charming place at Tarpon Springs, and who insisted on adding
needed supplies to our limited store, and little comforts to our else
rather barren cabins. We had reason enough to be grateful to them
during our long continued stay in the more inaccessible waters of the
farther South.

In addition to Mrs. Cushing, myself, and Messrs. Sawyer, Sayford and
Bergmann, my crew consisted of Antonio Gomez, Sailing-Master;
Thomas Brady, Mate ; Alfred Hudson, Robert Clark and Frank Barnes,
Sailors and Excavators ; George Gause, Chief Excavator ; George
Hudson (colored), Cook ; George Dorsett (colored), Steward ; and I
later employed John Calhoun continuously, and other workmen, from
time to time, to assist in the excavations. I make mention of the names
of these men in order to express appreciation of the faithful and patient
manner in which they performed their duties and assisted me throughout
many trying days of labor in the water-soaked, foul-smelling muck and
peat beds of Marco and neighboring keys. My acknowledgments are
especially due to Gause, young Hudson, and Clark, who continually
worked in the muck holes side by side with Mr. Bergmann and myself,
and to whose painstaking care and attention it is due that many a fragile
treasure was saved from destruction.

The voyage from Tarpon Springs to Marco, including a stop at Pine
Island for mail and for taking in of fuel and water, occupied less than
three days, and as there was a steady Gulf breeze and the tides were
unusually high, we were able to make the difficult pass into Marco Inlet
without hindrance. There, just to the northeast of the key, we
anchored at a sufficient distance off shore to protect us measurably from
the mosquitoes, and there our little craft rode at anchor during the two
months occupied in the excavations and in my various expeditions to
surrounding keys—for these were made in a light-draught, double-
sailed sharpie, that had been fitted up and generously turned over for
our use by Mr. Cheney.

Immediately on arriving at Key Marco, I made arrangements with
Captain Collier whereby, in return for saving such muck as we should

turn over in our excavations, I would be permitted to retain all objects discovered, and if desirable, to exploit the little triangular "Court of the Pile Dwellers" from border to border. It lay, as I have said, close alongside the sea-wall at the southwestern edge of the key and just below a succession of shell benches, themselves formerly abandoned and filled-up courts of a similar character. The side opposite the sea-wall, that is on the east, was formed by an extended ridge—scarcely less high than the sea-wall itself, and likewise composed of well-compacted shells. Around the upper end, and down the outer side of this ridge, led—as indicated in plan, Plate XXXI—an inlet canal, bordered by similar ridges beyond, and joined by an outlet canal at the lower end—that continued through various low-banked enclosures in the mangrove swamps toward the south, quite down to the terminus of the sea-wall itself.

The entire court was thickly overgrown with mangrove trees, underneath which also thickly grew, to a uniform height of six or eight inches, bright green aquatic weeds and mangrove shoots. Since the interior of this artificial and filled-up bayou was still not above the level of the surrounding tide-swept mangrove swamps through which the canals led, it lay almost continually under water, and its excavation looked at first to be almost impossible, and at best a most formidable undertaking. It would be necessary to cut away and uproot the mangroves and in some way to remove the water that filled to overflowing the excavations which had formerly been made, and thus covered the entire court. To begin, I had a few of the trees cleared away from the outer and southwesterly corner, and opposite my old excavation in sections 34, 44, had a trench cut through the sea-wall to as great a depth as possible without letting water in from the bay outside. I then had a long trough of ship planks constructed and placed on stakes driven deep into the muck bed, so that one end rested over the excavation and the other, lower end, in the mouth of the sluice-way through the sea-wall. Then laying heavy planks over the boggy surface to furnish foothold for the men, I set them at work baling out the old excavation with buckets. It was at first like trying to bale out the sea itself, for water flowed in as fast as taken out ; but after two or three hours of steady work, it began to lower, not only in the excavation, but over the entire court, and toward evening it became possible to even begin the extension of this original excavation in the direction of the cleared corner of the court. On the following morning, however, there was almost as much water in the excavation thus enlarged, and elsewhere, as on the previous day ; but it was much sooner disposed of by baling and by the banking up of the place last excavated, and I soon found that by thus proceeding each morning for a couple of hours more or less, the water could be kept sufficiently low to enable us, working in sections, or bins as it were (roughly corresponding to those shown in the plan), to excavate the entire place. Yet, even thus, much of our search in the lower depths had to be made merely by feeling with the fingers.

I deem it unnecessary to give further details of our operations, save to say that three or four of us worked side by side in each section, digging inch by inch, and foot by foot, horizontally through the muck and rich lower strata, standing or crouching the while in puddles of mud and water ; and as time went on we were pestered morning and evening by swarms and clouds of mosquitoes and sand-flies, and during the midhours of the day, tormented by the fierce tropic sun heat, pouring down, even thus early in the season into this little shut-up hollow among the breath-less mangroves. After the first day's work, however, I was left no longer in doubt as to the unique outcome of our excavations, or as to the desir-ability of searching through the entire contents of the court, howsoever difficult the task might prove to be ; for relics not only of the kind already described, but of new and even more interesting varieties, began at once to be found, and continued to be found increasingly as we went on day after day, throughout the entire five weeks of our work in this one little place. I may be permitted to add that never in all my life, despite the sufferings this labor involved, was I so fascinated with or interested in anything so much, as in the finds thus daily revealed. Partaking of my enthusiasm, the men, too, soon became so absorbed that they actually hated to see the sun go down and to thus be compelled to abandon their work even until the coming of another day.

As the northwesterly half of the court became cleared of its contents, and the bottom was thus more and more revealed, we found that it was generally concave, or perhaps I may say, tray-shaped ; that is, compara-tively shallow at the sides—not more than from eighteen inches to three feet deep—but throughout the middle and thence toward the mouths of the two canals, from four-and-a-half to five-and-a-half feet deep. Extending along the bottom, in toward this central deeper portion, from both the southwesterly and northwesterly margins at about equidistant intervals of twenty feet, were several straight, low benches or tongues, of compacted shell and tough clay-marl (shown in plan, Plate XXXI), from twenty-five to thirty feet long and from eight to twelve feet wide, level on top and built to a height gradually increasing from a few inches, where they joined the boundary banks, to nearly two feet at their rounded ends, so as to form low, originally submerged, slightly inclining piers, as it were. Along the opposite or eastern side was a similar, although con-tinuous bench, uniformly some fifteen feet wide from its rounded upper end just below the mouth of the inlet canal, to a point about thirty feet below, whence it gradually narrowed to a width of less than eight feet at its lower end near the mouth of the outlet canal. Finally, across the extreme upper end or corner of the court, that is just to the left of and above the mouth of the same inlet canal, extended a like, although slightly wider and shorter bench. Thus the whole central portion of the court, as well as the spaces between the tongues or benches, had been left open and deep, as if for the free passage of canoes. Along the sides and around the ends of these in-reaching benches of shell and clay, occurred numerous piles of various lengths, all, however, comparatively short, blunt-pointed at their lower ends, and either squared or else rudely notched at their upper ends—some of them slantingly bored down the sides—and there occurred also many stakes and timbers; as though these benches had been built to serve actually as piers or the foundations for long, pile-supported quays or scaffolds; upon which, I concluded—from the character of many lesser remains that we continually found—had been constructed, side by side all around the court, comparatively long, narrow, and low, thatched and latticed houses. At any rate it was over and around these benches that the principal finds, inclusive of numerous household articles, were made.

The surface deposit throughout the entire court consisted of a stratum of spongy black or dark brown muck, permeated by both rotting and living rootlets. It was, as shown in section on Plate XXXI, thin at the margins, but eighteen or twenty inches thick throughout the middle. Below this was a somewhat thicker stratum of brownish gray peaty marl, soft, tremulous, exceedingly foul-smelling, and rich in the best preserved relics we discovered. This stratum directly overlaid and surrounded the benches I have described. Finally underneath it, between the benches and throughout the middle of the court, was a less well-defined layer of less peaty marl, intermixed with shells and other *débris*, and also with abundant ancient remains—which, indeed, we continued to encounter even in the underlying, comparatively firm shell and clay-marl bottom. This, however, although nearly a foot and a half thick, we could not venture to excavate, since the slightest opening made through it into the sandy reef below let in a steady stream of water from the sea.

The objects found by us in these deposits were in various conditions of preservation, from such as looked fresh and almost new, to such as could scarcely be traced through or distinguished from the briny peat mire in which they were embedded. They consisted of wood, cordage and like perishable materials associated with implements and ornaments of more enduring substances, such as shell, bone and horn—for only a few shaped of stone were encountered during the entire search.

Articles of wood far outnumbered all others. I was astounded to soon find that many of these had been painted with black, white, gray-blue, and brownish-red pigments; and that while the wood itself was so decayed and soft that in many cases it was difficult to distinguish the fibre of even large objects of it, either by sight or by touch, from the muck and peat in which they were unequally distributed, but now more or less integrated; yet when discoverable in time to be cautiously uncovered and washed off by the splashing or trickling of water over them from a sponge, their forms appeared not only almost perfect, but also deceptively well preserved, so that I at first thought we might, with sufficient care, recover nearly all of them uninjured. This was especially true of such as had been decorated with the pigments; for owing to the presence in these pigments of a gum-like and comparatively insoluble sizing, the coatings of color were often relatively better preserved than the woody substance they covered, and enabled us the more readily to distinguish the outlines of these painted objects—when else some had been partially destroyed or altogether missed—and also enabled us to take them up on broad, flat shovels, and to more deliberately divest them of the muck and peat that so closely clung to them.

Some of the things thus recovered could be preserved by very slow drying, but it soon became evident that by far the greater number of them could not be kept intact. No matter how perfect they were at first, they warped, shrunk, split, and even checked across the grain, like old charcoal, or else were utterly disintegrated on being exposed to the light and air if only for a few hours. Thus, despite the fact that after removing the surface muck from the sections, we dug only with little hand-trowels and flexible-pronged garden claws—and, as I have said before, with our fingers—yet fully twenty-five per cent. of these ancient articles in wood and other vegetal material were destroyed in the search; and again, of those found and removed, not more than one-half retained their original forms unaltered for more than a few days.

Unique to archæology as these things were, it was distressing to feel that even by merely exposing and inspecting them, we were dooming so many of them to destruction, and to think that of such as we could temporarily recover only the half could be preserved as permanent examples of primitive art.

I sought by every means at our disposal to remedy these difficulties, but I soon found that the time thus required, and the cost of additional preservatives—if such could, indeed, be found, for ordinary glue, shellac, and silicate of soda, proved to be comparatively inefficient—would increase the cost of our operations considerably beyond my original estimates upon which appropriation had been made.

In this extremity I wrote to Major Powell, asking for suggestions as to methods for preserving our finds, and at the same time to Doctor Pepper, urging an additional appropriation. I was loath to do this, being well aware that the funds at the disposal of the Department he represented were already overtaxed by the many explorations progressing under his direction in other parts of the world. My relief of mind may be better imagined than described, when I say that as speedily as the mails could bring a letter from Doctor Pepper, he assured me that my operations looking toward the proper completion of our excavations and preservation of our collections would be supported to the extent required. It was not until afterward that I learned how a friend whom to know is to honor and revere, a friend to education and scientific research and human need wherever found, Mrs. Phebe A. Hearst, had, as a member of the Department of Archæology and Palæontology, come to our rescue. The gratification I feel in announcing the augmented success of our researches, thenceforward, is enhanced by the thought that I may here say how much this success was due to her instant recognition of the promise and significance of our finds.

Whilst I was still awaiting reply from my Director, Major J. W. Powell, and wondering as to the possible outcome of our undertakings— as to whether the extent of the field we had opened could, with such relatively imperfect results as I then looked for, be sufficiently represented to the scientific world to command due recognition of its significance ethnographically, I was happily honored by an unannounced visit from Major Powell himself. Instead of replying to my letter, he had immediately set out to visit us, in order to aid personally and on the spot in devising means for the preservation, if not of the collections, at least of a full and adequate record of our finds and discoveries. I had, therefore, the combined pleasure and advantage of exhibiting to him, alike the field of my observations and the results of our researches therein, and of gaining from him the approval of his trusted judgment as to not only these results, but also as to the methods whereby they had been achieved.

At this time, however, the season of rain and excessive heat had set in, rendering it certain that the days of the expedition in that section were numbered. Therefore after carefully inspecting our collections, Key Marco, and other typical shell settlements in that portion of the Ten Thousand Islands, Major Powell urgently counseled me to confine operations thenceforward to the completion of excavations in this one little court of the pile dwellers, and therewith to close for the season a work which he again assured me was of unusual archæologic significance and capable, he believed, of indefinite extension.

Thus aided and encouraged by my superiors, I persisted, notwithstanding the more or less destructive nature of our researches, if only in order that we might secure the fullest possible data. Fortunately we were in the end able not only to enlarge and complete our collections of photographic records, sketches, surveys and other field memoranda, but also to secure and bring away, in measurably good condition, more than a thousand of these precious examples of prehistoric art in perishable materials, not to mention many hundreds of examples in more durable substances such as shell, bone and horn.

I must further state that the various ancient artifacts we found in the muck, occurred at unequal depths and in all sorts of positions and relations. There were a few groups of utensils, for example, that obviously belonged together, like mortar cups and pestles, and sets of tools that were still associated ; and there were also some few bundles or packs of ceremonial óbjects, apparently, which when found still remained almost intact ; that is, their wrappings of reed matting, or neat swathings of flag or palmetto leaves still, looked fresh, actually green, in some cases ; but on close examination they proved always to be pulpy with decay and impossible of removal. These packs and assemblages or bunches of related things, however, did not present the appearance of deliberate deposition. They looked as though they had fallen and sunken where we found them—some being upside down—as though they had been hanging, or else lying, tucked away in the houses or on the scaffolds above, and had been washed out from or off of them into the water alongside and below, had become water-logged and had gradually been covered by mud and other *débris* and by the vegetal and other deposits we found them in.

By far the greater number of objects were, however, promiscuously scattered—although, as I have said, more abundant between and around the ends or along the edges of the low, submerged benches I have described, than elsewhere. Not a few of them—and this was especially the case with long and originally more or less fragile articles like spear-shafts and stays—appeared to have been broken in falling. Occasionally we found fragments separated by considerable distance which, when brought together, fitted perfectly. Not a few of the piles were thus broken, and many of the lesser timbers; while larger timbers, like the comparatively gigantic sill, which lay along the·edge of the northern bench (in sections 29, 39, 40), were absolutely intact. They were excellent examples of primitive joinery; yet so soft and pulpy, as a rule, that on account of their great size and weight, we were unable to bring them away, or even, without destroying, to disturb them. Some of the broad, flat, notched staves—which I judged from considerations later offered had been used as symbolic ancestral tablets, probably attached to the gables of houses, or set up in altars—were lying on their edges; while flat boards sometimes stood on end, and other long, slender articles, stood slantingly upward, the lowermost ends or edges firmly stuck in the clay-marl of the bottom. This was the case, for example, with the beautifully shaped and pointed paddle which we found near the mouth of the upper or inlet canal. Its sharp point was slantingly and deeply embedded in the mud, while its long handle reached obliquely up nearly to the surface of the muck, and was there, as may be seen by examination of the specimen itself (or of Fig. 8, in Plate XXXII), burned off slantingly on a line that must have corresponded to the original level of the water, for at this point other charred specimens occurred, as though here fire had added its destructiveness to the storm that demolished the buildings or scaffolds from which all these things seemed to have fallen.

From the fact that many of the objects lay suspended, as it were, in the mud *above* the bottom, I judged that when these remains were thrown down into the little water court, the spaces between the house-benches and around the borders of the quays at least, must have been already choked up somewhat with *débris* or refuse and slime or mud; for out in the middle of the court where the deep open space occurred throughout the channel between the two canals, little was found in the way of art remains, except such as lay directly upon, or very near to, the bottom.

It may be seen that by a study of the distribution of these remains it was easy to determine what had been the original average depth of the water within the court, or at any rate, its depth at the time when these things found their way into it, and to determine also many other features of the place, interesting as details and important too, as substantiating various inferences I have ventured to give above. But as a careful study of the collections themselves repeats to a great extent this story of our field observations, I will make haste to present a descriptive account of the various classes of these.

ANCIENT ARTIFACTS FROM THE COURT OF THE PILE DWELLERS.

Piles, Timbers, etc.—None of the piles found by us exceeded six and a half feet in length. Indeed, the greater number of them were less than three and a half feet long. These shorter piles were nearly always made of palmetto wood, were not round, but broad, or somewhat flattened, although the edges were rounded. They were tapered toward the bottom and bluntly pointed, rudely squared or hollowed out at the tops as though to support round, horizontal timbers ; and they were bored or notched slantingly here and there through the edges, as though for the reception of rounded braces or cross-stays of poles or saplings, abundant pieces of which were found. Some of the piles were worn at the points or lower ends, as though they had rested upon, but had not been driven into, the solid shell and clay-marl benches. They had apparently, on the contrary, been quite rigidly fastened to the horizontal timbers or frameworks of the quays or scaffolds they held up—by means of the staysticks—like pegs or pointed feet, so that as long as the water remained low, they would support these house scaffolds above it, as well as if driven into the benches, but when the waters rose, the entire structures would also slightly rise, or at any rate not be violently wrenched from their supports, as would inevitably have been the case had these been firmly fixed below. The longer piles were, on the contrary, round. They were somewhat smaller, quite smoothly finished, and had been, if one might judge by their more pointed and yet roughened or frayed appearance at both ends, actually driven into the bottom. It therefore appeared to me that they had been made so as to be thus driven into the edges of the benches at either side of the peg-supported platforms, in order to keep these from swerving in case an unusual rise in the waters caused them to float. There were other pieces equally long, but broken off near their points. They were slightly grooved at the upper ends and tied around with thick, well-twisted ropes or cables made of cypress bark and palmetto fibre, as though they had served as mooring-posts, probably for the further securing of the ends of the partially movable platforms—else they had not been so violently wrenched as to break them at the points—for some of them were more than four inches in diameter, and were made of tough mangrove and buttonwood or iron-wood. The side-posts or stay-stakes were, on the contrary, of spruce or pine, and were, as I have said, finished to a nicety, as though to offer no resistance to the rise and fall of the big, partially floating quays between them. Around the great log or sill of cypress, mentioned as lying along the edge of the northern bench (it was uniformly nine inches in diameter, fourteen feet eleven inches in length, carefully shaved to shape and finished evidently with shark-tooth blades and shell scrapers, and was moreover, like the piles, socketed and notched or bored along its sides) were many of these piles, both short and long; and overlying the sill, as well as on either side of it, I found abundant broken timbers, poles, and traces of wattled cane matting as well as quantities of interlaced or latticed saplings—laths evidently, for they seemed to have been plastered with a clay and ash cement—and quantities also of yellow marsh-grass thatch, some of it alluringly fresh, other portions burnt to black masses of cinder. Here and elsewhere along the edges of the benches occurred fire-hardened cement or mud hearth-plastering, mingled with ashes and charcoal—which indeed occurred more or less abundantly everywhere, together with refuse, consisting not only of broken and sometimes scorched animal bones and shells, but also of the charred remains of vegetable and fruit foods. Among these remains and the more artificial objects that were associated with them we continually encountered incipient or unfinished pieces—blocked-out trays or toy canoes, untrimmed adze and axe handles, uncompleted tablets, etc., and all this evidenced to me that the place was indeed a site of former daily occupation.

Furniture, etc.—Here and there were found curious wooden seats—more or less like ancient Antillean stools, as may be seen in Fig. 7, Pl. XXXIV—flat slabs of wood from a foot to more than two feet in length, slightly hollowed on top from end to end as well as from side to side, with rounded bottoms and substantial, prong-like pairs of feet near either end, from two to three inches long. Some of these stools had the feet level; others, so spread and beveled that they would exactly fit the hollow bottoms of canoes. Others still were smaller than those I have mentioned, so diminutive, in fact, that they could have served no purpose else, it seemed to me, than that of head-rests or pillow-supports. We found, indeed, although we were unable to preserve any of them, examples of what might have been the pillows used in connection with these rests. They were taperingly cylindrical, made of fine rushes, and showed a continuous four-ply plat, so that, like cassava strainers, they were flexible and compressible, yet springy, and they had probably been filled with Florida moss or deer hair, which filling had, however, long since disappeared save for a mushy residuum. Portions of mats, some thick, as though for use as rugs, others enveloping various objects, and others still of shredded bark in strips so thin and flat and closely platted that they might well have served as sails, were frequently discovered. Yet except for masses of the peat or mud upon which the remains of this matting lay and which therefore when dry showed traces of its beautifully and variously formed plies, naught of them could be preserved. It was obvious, however, that the peoples who had inhabited the court understood well, not only platting, but weaving and basketry-making too.

Pottery and Utensils.—A few examples of pottery were discovered lying always on or near the bottom, and with one exception invariably broken. All of these vessels, notwithstanding the fact that some of them had their rims more or less decorated, showed evidence of having been used as cooking bowls or pots. Associated with them were household utensils—spoons made from bivalves, ladles made from the greater halves of hollowed-out well-grown conch shells; and cups, bowls, trays and mortars of wood. These latter were in greatest variety and abundance. They ranged in size from little hemispherical bowls or cups two and a half or three inches in diameter, to great cypress tubs more than two feet in depth, tapering, flat-bottomed, and correspondingly wide at the tops. The smaller mortar-cups were marvels of beauty and finish as a rule, and lying near them and sometimes even within them, were still found their appropriate pestles or crushers—as is shown in Fig. 5, Pl. XXXIV. The smaller mortars and pestles, like the one illustrated, seemed to have been personal property, as though they had belonged to individuals and had been used in the crushing of berries and tubers, and perhaps cunti-root; as well as in other ways, that is, in the service, rather than merely in the general preparation, of food.

The trays were also very numerous and exceedingly interesting; comparatively shallow, oval in outline and varying from a length of six and a half or seven inches and a width of four or five inches, to a length of not less than five feet and a width of quite two feet. The ends of these trays were narrowed and truncated to form handles, the upper faces of which were usually decorated with neatly cut-in disc-like or semilunar figures or depressions. Looking at the whole series of them secured by us—no fewer than thirty in all—I was impressed with their general resemblance to canoes, their almost obvious derivation from such, as though through a sort of technologic inheritance they had descended from the vessels which had brought not only the first food, and the first supplies of water, to these outlying keys, but also the first dwellers thereon as well.

Navigating Apparatus and Fishing Gear. — This inference was strengthened by the discovery here and there of actual toy canoes. That they had been designed as toys was evident from the fact that some were not only well finished, but considerably worn by use. There were six or seven of these, and while they generally conformed to a single type, that is the dugout, they differed very materially in detail. Three of them were comparatively flat-bottomed. One, about five inches in length by two in breadth of beam and an inch in depth, was shaped precisely like a neat punt or flat-bottomed row boat—Fig. 7, Pl. XXXII. Both ends were somewhat squared, but the stern was wider than the prow, and above the stern was a little protuberance, indicating that such had been used in guiding, and perhaps as well in sculling, little light draught vessels like this, obviously designed, my sailors thought, for the navigation of shallow streams, inlets, bayous, and the canals. Another of these flat-bottomed little toy boats was much sharper and higher at the stem and stern, had very low gunwales, and was generally narrower in proportion to its length, and enlarged would have been admirably adapted to swift tidal currents, or to the running of low breakers. Yet another looked like a clumsy craft for the bearing over shoals of heavy loads or burdens. It was comparatively wide, and its ends also quite broad. All except one of these, I observed, were decorated at one end or both, with the same sort of semilunar or disc-like devices, that were observable on the trays—as may be seen by an examination of Fig, 6, Pl. XXXII. Two others of the toy canoes (one of which is here figured as just referred to) were not more than three inches broad by nearly two feet in length, gracefully and slenderly formed, tapered cleanly toward the forward ends, which were high and very narrow, yet square at the sterns, which were also high. We found them almost in juxtaposition near the midmost of the western benches. Little sticks and slight shreds of twisted bark were lying across them and indicated to me that they had once been lashed together, and, as a more finished and broken spar-like shaft lay near by, I was inclined to believe that they represented the sea-going craft of the ancient people here ; that the vessels in which these people had navigated the high seas had been made double—of canoes lashed together, catamaran fashion—and propelled not only with paddles, but also, perhaps, by means of sails, made probably from the thin two-ply kind of bark matting I have before described, of which there were abundant traces near the midchannel, associated with cordage and with a beautifully regular, much worn and polished spar. At any rate, the natives of these South Florida seas and of the West Indies are mentioned by early writers as having navigated fearlessly in their cypress canoes ; as having sometimes crossed the Gulf itself, and as having used in these long cruises sails of some simple sort. Jonathan Dickinson, in his quaint volume entitled *God's Protecting Providence Man's Surest Help and Defence*, etc.—one of the first books published in this city, by the way—narrates how, just two hundred years ago, he and his companion voyagers were shipwrecked on the Florida Gulf shore. He clearly describes such a double canoe as we found the toy remains of, when he tells how a Cacique, into whose hands they fell, went to wrest back the plunder that had been taken from them by earlier captors. The Cacique—to quote the author freely—came home in great state He was nearly nude and triumphantly painted red, and sitting cross-legged on their ship's chest, that stood on a platform midway over *two canoes lashed together with poles.* He maintained a fierce expression of countenance and looked neither to the left nor to the right, but merely exclaimed " wow " when they greeted him from the shore ; and, after landing, proceeded—the author adds rather ruefully—to appropriate the contents of the chest to himself.

Two tackle-blocks, real prehistoric pulleys, that we found, may have pertained to such canoes as these. Each was three inches long, oval, one side rounded, the other cut in at the edges, or rabbetted so to say. The tenon-like portion was gouged out midway, transversely pierced, and furnished with a smooth peg or pivot over which the cordage turned. I have already mentioned the finding of a paddle near the mouth of the inlet canal—which is shown in Fig. 8, Pl. XXXII. It was neatly shaped, the handle round and lengthy, although burned off at the end, and the blade also long, leaf-shaped, and tapered to a sharp point, convex or beveled on one side, flat or slightly spooned or concave on the other. The splintered gunwales and a portion of the prow of a long, light cypress-wood canoe, and various fragments of a large but clumsier boat of some soft spongy kind of wood—gumbo-limbo, probably—were found down toward the middle of the court. Not far from the remains of these I came across an ingenious anchor. It consisted of a bunch of large triton-shells roughly pierced and lashed together with tightly twisted cords of bark and fibre so that the long, spike-like ends stood out radiatingly, like the points of a star. They had all been packed full of sand and cement, so as to render them, thus bunched, sufficiently heavy to hold a good-sized boat. Near the lower edge of the eastern bench lay another anchor. It was made of flat, heart-shaped stones, similarly perforated and so tied and cemented together with fibre and a kind of red vegetable gum and sand, that the points stood out radiatingly in precisely the same manner. Yet another anchor was formed from a single boulder of coraline limestone a foot in diameter. Partly by nature, more by art, it was shaped to resemble the head of a porpoise perforated for attachment at the eye-sockets. Balers made from large conch shells crushed in at one side, or of wood, shovel shaped, or else scoop shaped, with handles turned in, were abundant ; as were also nets of tough fibre, both coarse and fine, knitted quite as is the common netting of our own fisherman to-day, in form of fine-meshed, square dip-nets, and of coarse-meshed, comparatively large and long gill-nets. To the lower edges of these, sinkers made from thick, roughly perforated umboidal bivalves, tied together in bunches, or else from chipped and notched fragments of heavy clam shells, were attached, while to the upper edges, floats made from gourds, held in place by fine net-lashings, or else from long sticks or square-ended blocks, were fastened. Around the avenues of the court I was interested to find netting of coarser cordage weighted with unusually large-sized or else heavily bunched sinkers of shell, and supplied at the upper edges with long, delicately tapered gumbo-limbo float-pegs, those of each set equal in size, each peg thereof partially split at the larger end, so as to clamp double half-turns or ingeniously knotted hitches of the neatly twisted edges-cords with which all were made fast to the nets. Now these float pegs, of which many sets were secured, varying from three and a half to eight inches in length of pegs, were so placed on the nets, that in consequence of their tapering forms they would turn against the current of the tide whichever way it flowed, and would continuously bob up and down on the ripples, however slight these were, in such manner as to frighten the fish that had been driven, or had passed over them at high tide, when, as the tide lowered, they naturally tried to follow it. In connection with these nets we found riven stays, usually of cypress or pine, such as might have been used in holding them upright. Hence I inferred that they had been stretched across the channels not only of the actual water courts of residence, like this, but, probably also, of the surrounding fish-pounds ; and if so, that the supply of fresh fish must always have been abundant with the ancient inhabitants, both near at hand in these enclosures, as well as even among the quays of the actual residence courts.

We found four or five fish-hooks. The shanks or stems of these were about three inches long, shaped much like those of our own, but made from the conveniently curved main branches of the forked twigs of some tough springy kind of wood. These were cut off at the forks in such manner as to leave a portion of the stems to 'serve as butts, which were girdled and notched in, so that the sharp, barbed points of deer bone, which were about half as long as the shanks and leaned in toward them, could be firmly attached with sinew and black rubber-gum cement. The stems were neatly tapered toward the upper ends, which terminated in slight knobs, and to these, lines—so fine that only traces of them could be recovered—were tied by half-hitches, like the turns of a bow string. Little plug-shaped floats of gumbo-limbo wood, and sinkers made from the short thick columellæ of turbinella shells—not shaped and polished like the highly finished plummet-shaped pendants we secured in great numbers, but with the whorls merely battered off— seemed to have been used with these hooks and lines. That they were designed for deep-sea fishing was indicated by the occurrence of flat reels or spools shaped precisely like fine-toothed combs divested of their inner teeth There were also shuttles or skein-holders of hard wood, six or seven inches long, with wide semicircular crotches at the ends. But these may have served in connection with a double kind of barb, made from two notched or hooked crochet-like points or prongs of deer bone, that we found attached with fibre cords to a concave round-ended plate, an inch wide and three inches long, made from the pearly nacre of a pinna shell. Since several of these shining, ovoid plates were procured, I regarded them as possibly "baiting-spoons," and this one with the barbed contrivance, as some kind of trolling gear, though it may, as the sailors thought, have been a " pair of grains," or may, like the hook proper, have been used for deep-sea fishing. Aside from these few articles, no other fishing tackle for use in the open waters was found ; barbed harpoons being conspicuously absent. This led to the supposition that the ancient inhabitants had depended chiefly upon the pounds and water courts, whence with their nets they could at any time have readily drawn greater numbers of the fish for their supply.

Tools and Implements.—The working parts of the various instruments of handicraft that we found were not of stone, but almost exclusively of hard organic substances—shell, bone, horn, and teeth—principally those of sharks—with their various kinds of wooden appurtenances or haftings, sometimes intact, sometimes merely indicated by the presence of fragments or traces—distinct enough, but too often wholly un-recoverable. In most cases these diverse parts were still in their origi-nal relation to one another, although, as a rule, the lashings by which they had been bound together—having consisted, as could plainly be seen by impressions left even in the surrounding mud, of rawhide thongs or of twisted sinew or fishgut—had wholly dissolved, or else re-mained merely as a dubious sort of gelatinous mass or slime. Such bind-ings had, however, in many instances been reinforced with cements of one kind or another—a sticky red substance, the stain only of which remained—or else rubber-gum, asphaltum, or a combination of rosin and beeswax and rubber, which still endured and retained perfect impres-sions of the fastening cords, whether coarse thongs or finely twisted threads.

We exercised great caution in keeping related parts together, and succeeded thus in recovering quite a number of examples of each of the many types most characteristic of the technical arts of the keys.

Large clam shells, deeply worn at the backs, as well as showing much use at the edges, seemed to have served both as scrapers and as digging implements or hoes ; for some of them had been hafted by clamping curved sticks over the hinge and over the point at the apex or umbo—where it showed wear—precisely in such manner as LeMoine seems to have attempted to show in his representation—published in De Bry and other early works—of Indians planting corn.

Picks, hammers, adzes and gouges made from almost entire conch shells were found, handles and all, in relatively perfect condition and in considerable numbers. As may be seen by reference to the accom-panying illustration, Fig. 1, Pl. XXXII, the conch-shell heads of these tools were most ingeniously hafted. The whorl was usually battered away on the side toward the mouth, so as to expose the columella. The lip was roundly notched or pierced, and the back whorl also perforated oppositely. Thus the stick or handle could be driven into these perfora-tions, past the columella in such manner that it was sprung or clamped firmly into place. Nevertheless it was usually further secured with raw-hide thongs—now mere jelly—passed through one or two additional per-forations in the head, and around both the stick and the columella. The spike-like ends of the columellæ were so shaped as to form either long, sharp-pointed picks, flat, small-faced hammers or battering tools, adzes with very narrow bits, or gouges. The edges of the gouges were wider than those of the other tools, more of the wings of the shells having been left on the ends of the columellæ and these half-hollow points hav-ing been simply ground off obliquely. I made a tool of this description, which worked admirably on the hardest wood I could get ; and retained its edge amazingly well. Several very ingenious hacking tools or broad-axes had been made merely from the lips and portions of the outer or body-whorls of these conchs. They were simply notched at the ends so as to receive correspondingly grooved or notched sticks which were bound to their inner sides with thongs passed around the ends and over the backs. The wide, curved, natural edge of the lips, had then been neatly sharpened. Among the blocked-out pieces of wood so frequently found were examples of the work done not only with these hollow hacking tools, but also with the chisel- and gouge-pointed implements I have described, as was clearly shown by the results of my experiments. In addition to these cutting tools, celts, or rather celt-shaped, but curved adze-blades, two of them in connection with their handles—which were made from forked branches, one limb cut short and shouldered to receive the blade, the other left long, to serve as the handle—were also recovered. True celts were found too, made from the heavy columellæ of triton shells. One of them was accompanied by a pierced handle, the most elaborately decorated object of its kind thus far found in our country. It was superbly carved from end to end with curved volute-like decorations, concentric circles, ovals, and overpliced as well as parallel lines, regularly divided by encircling bands, as though derived from ornate lashings; while the head or extreme end was notched around for the attachment of plumes or tassels, and the opposite or handle-end furnished with an eyelet to facilitate suspension. Numbers of carving adzes, as was plainly indicated by marks of their work on both finished and unfinished objects, were also secured, quite in their entirety. Each consisted of a curved or crozier-shaped handle of hardwood about a foot in length, sharply crooked toward the head, which consisted of a perfectly fitted, carved, polished and socketed section of deer horn. The socket at the point of this deer-horn head was deep, transverse, and so shaped as to receive and retain measurably well, little blades made either from bits of shell, the sharp ventral valves of oysters—of which kind numerous worn-out examples were gathered—or sometimes, from very large shark or alligator teeth. These peculiar little hand-adzes—that resembled some of those one may see pictured in the figures of mask-carvers in Central American and Mexican codices—seem to have been, judged from the work performed with them, among the most perfect implements possessed by the inhabitants. That they were favorite tools also, was shown by the fact that many of them were elaborately carved. All had eyes, mostly protuberant, just above the sockets, and one, for example, was slightly crooked from side to side, and shaped to represent a fanged serpent; another had carved near its head, a surprisingly realistic horned-deer's head, and yet another was surmounted by the figure of a gopher or rodent gnawing at a stick—see Fig. 2, Pl. XXXII; and in these forms I did not fail to recognize the association that was attempted, by this sort of decoration between the carvings, and the functions of these biting or gnawing implements, so to call them.

Of course scrapers and shavers of various kinds abounded. Some, of large, finely-ribbed, serrated bivalves—varieties of pectunculus—were perforated at the apices, in order that a loop might be attached to them to facilitate handling. Others were made from the valves of tide-water unios, or sun-clams, so called, and showed no other art than that of having been keenly sharpened at the edges, and of the wear which had resulted from use. The most elaborate objects of this kind were, however, certain flat-hinged bivalves or arca shells, about three and a half or four inches long. The umboidal apices of these had been broken away and strips of bark, and in at least one case, broad straps of a kind of leather, had been so passed back and forth through the apertures, and platted along the hinges or straight backs, as to afford excellent grasp. All of them were crenulate at the edges and some of them were double, that is, made of two shells tightly tied together, one inside of the other, in such manner that a double edge was thereby secured. Several draw-knives made from split leg-bones of the deer sharpened to beveled edges from the inside; some ingenious shaving-knives, made from the outer marginal whorls of the true conchs—the thick indented or toothed lips of which formed their backs or handles, the thin but strong whorl-walls being sharpened to keen straight edges—completed the list of scraping and planing tools.

Cutting and carving knives of shark's teeth, varying in size from tiny straight points to curved blades nearly an inch in length and in width of base, were found by hundreds. Some were associated with their handles. These were of two classes. The greater number of them consisted of shafts from five to seven inches in length by not more than half or three-quarters of an inch in diameter at their thickest portions. Some were slightly curved, others straight, some pointed, others squared at the smaller ends. All were furnished with nocks at the lower ends—which were also a little tapered—for the reception of the hollow bases of the tooth-blades that had been lashed to them and cemented with black gum. Not a few of these doubly-tapered little handles were marvels of finish, highly polished, and some of them were carved or incised with involuted circlets or kwa-like decorations, or else with straight or spiral-rayed rosettes and concentric circles, at the upper ends, as though these had been used as stamps in the finishing of certain kinds of work. The other class of handles was much more various, and was designed for receiving one or more of the shark-tooth blades, not at the extremities, but at the sides of the ends, some transversely, others laterally. They were nearly all carved ; a few of them most elaborately ; and they ranged in length from the width of the palm of the hand to five or six inches, being adapted for use not only as carvers, but also, probably— such as had single crossblades—as finishing adzes.

Everywhere on the least finished surfaces of completed carvings, and on incipient works, not only in wood, but also in bone and horn, could be seen distinctive marks left by the finely serrated edges of these more than half-natural carving tools. As soon as we had discovered a few of them I secured fresh teeth and experimentally made knives and cutters of the various kinds I have described. I found these diminutive shark-tooth blades—the one edge of each outwardly, the other inwardly, curved—by far the most effective primitive carving tools I had ever learned of, and therein perceived one of the principal causes of the pre-eminence of the ancient key dwellers in the wood carver's art, so constantly evidenced in our collections. There were girdling tools or saws —made from the sharp, flat-toothed lower jaws of king-fishes—into the hollow ends of which curved jaw-bones, the crudest of little handles had been thrust and tied through neat lateral perforations ; but these also had formed admirable tools, and I found not a few examples of work done with them, in the shape of round billets that had been severed by them and spirally haggled in such a way as to plainly illustrate the origin of one of the most frequent decorations we found on carved wood works, the spiral rosette just referred to. There were minute little bodkin-shaped chisels of bone and shell, complete in themselves ; and there were, of course, numerous awls and the like, made from bone, horn and fish spines. Rasps of very small, much worn and evidently most highly prized fragments of coral sandstone, as well as a few strips of carefully rolled-up shark skin, told the story of how the harder tools had been edged, and the polished wood-, and bone-work finished, here.

Weapons.—It was significant that no bows were discovered in any portion of the court, but of atlatls or throwing sticks, both fragmentary and entire, four or five examples were found. Two of the most perfect of these were also the most characteristic, since one was double-holed, the other single-holed. The first—which is shown in Fig. 4, Pl. XXXII— was some eighteen inches in length, delicate, slender, slightly curved and originally, quite springy. It was fitted with a short spur at the smaller end and was unequally spread or flanged at the larger or grasping end. The shaft-groove terminated in an ornamental device, whence a slighter crease led quite to the end of the handle, and the whole implement was delicately carved and engraved with edge-lines and when first taken from the muck exhibited a high polish and beautiful rosewood color. The other—shown in Fig. 3, Pl. XXXII—was somewhat longer, slightly thicker, wider shafted, more curved, and, as I have said before, furnished with only a single finger-hole. At the smaller end was a diminutive but very perfect carving of a rabbit, in the act of thumping, so placed that his erect tail formed the propelling-spur. This instrument also was fitted with a short shaft-groove and was carved and decorated with edge and side lines, and the handle-end was beautifully curved down and rounded so as to form a volute or rolled knob, giving it a striking resemblance to the ornate forms of the atlatl of Central America ; a resemblance that also applied somewhat to the double-holed specimen, and to various of the fragmentary spear-throwers. Arrows about four feet in length, perfectly uniform, pointed with hard wood, the shafts made either of a softer and lighter kind of wood or of cane, were found. The nocks of these were relatively large. This suggested that certain curved and shapely clubs, or rather wooden sabres —for they were armed along one edge with keen shark-teeth— might have been used not only for striking, but also for flinging such nocked spears or throwing-arrows. Each of these singular and superbly finished weapons was about three feet long. The handle or grip was straight ; thence the blade or shaft was gently curved downward and upward again to the end, which was obliquely truncated below, but terminated above in a creased or slightly bifurcated, spirally curved knob or volute like the end of a violin, and still more like the lower articulation of a human femur,—as may be seen by reference to Fig. 5, Pl. XXXII,—which the whole weapon resembled in general outline so strikingly that I was inclined to regard the type it represented as remotely derived from clubs originally made in imitation of thigh-bones. The handle was broader at the back than below, but neatly rounded, and the extreme end delicately flared to insure grasp. At both shank and butt of this grip, oblong holes had been bored obliquely through one side of the back for the attachment of a braided or twisted hand-loop or guard-cord, to still further secure hold. The back of the shaft, too, was wide, and sharp along the lateral edges, from both of which it was hollowed obliquely to the middle, the shallow V-shaped trough or groove thus formed reaching from the hilt to the turned-up end, where it terminated in a little semi-circular, sharp-edged cusp or spur in the central furrow at the base of the knob. The converging sides of the shaft were likewise evenly and sharply creased or fluted from the shank of the grip to the gracefully turned volutes at the sides of the knob. The blade proper, or lower edge, was comparatively thin, like a continuous slightly grooved tongue or an old-fashioned skate blade—save that it was obliquely square, not rounded, at the end. It was transversely pierced at regular intervals by semicircular perforations—twelve in all—beneath each of which the groove was deepened at two points to accommodate the blunt bifurcate roots of the large hooked teeth of the tiger- or "Man-Eater"- shark, with which the sabre was set ; so that, like the teeth of a saw, they would all turn one way, namely, toward the handle, as can be seen by reference to the enlarged sketch of one at the end of the figure. Finely twisted cords of sinew had been threaded regularly back and forth through these perforations and alternately over the wings of the shark teeth, so as to neatly bind each in its socket; and these lashings were reinforced with abundant black rubber-gum—to which their preservation was due.

Now the little cusp or sharp-edged spur at the end of the back-groove was so deeply placed in the crease of the knob that it could have served no practical purpose in a striking weapon. Yet, it was so shaped as to exactly fit the nock of a spear, and since by means of the guard cord, the handle could be grasped not only for striking, but, by shifting or reversing the hold, for hurling as well, I inferred that possibly the instrument had been used in part as an atlatl, in part as a kind of single-edged maquahuitl or blade-set sabre. It was, at any rate, a most formidable weapon and a superb example of primitive workmanship and ingenuity. There were other weapons somewhat like these. But they were only eight or nine inches in length, and were neither knobbed nor creased. They were, however, perforated at the backs for hand cords, and socketed below for six, instead of twelve teeth—set somewhat more closely together—and must have formed vicious slashers or rippers. Then there were certain split bear- and wolf-jaws—neatly cut off so as to leave the canines and two cuspids standing—which, from traces of cement on their bases and sides, appeared to have been similarly attached to curved clubs.

War clubs proper, that is, of wood only, were found in considerable variety. The most common form was that of the short, knobbed bludgeon. Another was nearly three feet long, the handle rounded, tapered, and furnished at the end with an eyelet for the wrist cord. The blade was flattish, widening to about three inches at the head, and it was laterally beveled from both sides to form blunt edges and was notched or roundly serrated, precisely as are some forms of Fijian and Caroline Island clubs. The type was obviously derived from some preëxisting kind of blade-set weapon. This was also true, in another way, of the most remarkable form of club we discovered. It was not quite two feet in length, and made of some dark-colored fine-grained kind of hard, heavy wood, exquisitely fashioned and finished. The handle was also round and tapering, the head flattened, symmetrically flaring and sharp-edged, the end square or but slightly curved, and terminating in a grooved knob or boss, to which tassel-cords had been attached. Just below the flaring head was a double blade, that is, a semilunar, sharp-edged projection on either side, giving the weapon the appearance of a double-edged battle-axe set in a broad-ended club, as indicated in outline *a* of Fig. 3, Pl. XXXV. This specimen was of especial interest, as it was the only weapon of its kind found, up to that time, in the United States; but was absolutely identical in outline with the so-called batons represented in the hands of warrior-figures delineated on the shell gorgets and copper plates found in the southern and central Mississippi mounds—as may be seen in the figure just referred to. It not only recalled these, but also typical double-bladed battle-axes or clubs of South and Central American peoples, from which type I regarded its form, although wholly of wood, as a derivative.

I must not fail to mention dirks or stilettos, made from the foreleg bones of deer, the grip ends flat, the blades conforming in curvature to the original lines of the bones from which they were made. One of them was exquisitely and conventionally carved at the hilt-end to represent the head of a buzzard or vulture, the which was no doubt held to be one of the gods of death by these primitive key-dwellers. There were also striking- and thrusting-weapons of slender make and of wood, save that they were sometimes tipped with deer horn or beautifully fashioned spurs of bone, but they were so fragmentary that I have thus far been unable to determine their exact natures.

Personal Ornaments and Paraphernalia.—Numerous objects of personal investure and adornment were collected. Aside from shell beads, pendants and gorgets, of kinds found usually in other southern relic sites, there were buttons, cord-knobs of large oliva-shells, and many little conical wooden plugs that had obviously formed the cores of tassels ; sliding-beads, of elaborately carved deer horn—for double cords— and one superb little brooch, scarcely more than an inch in width, made of hard wood, in representation of an angle-fish, the round spots on its back inlaid with minute discs of tortoise shell, the bands of the diminutive tail delicately and realistically incised, and the mouth, and a longitudinal eyelet as delicately incut into the lower side. There were very large labrets of wood for the lower lips, the shanks and insertions of which were small, and placed near one edge, so that the outer disc which had been coated with varnish or brilliant thin laminæ of tortoise shell, would hang low over the chin. There were lip-pins too ; and ear buttons, plates, spikes and plugs. The ear buttons were chiefly of wood, and were of special interest—the most elaborate articles of jewelry we found. They were shaped like huge cuff buttons—some, two inches in diameter, resembling the so-called spool-shaped copper bosses or ear ornaments of the mound builders (see *d* and Fig. 3, Pl. XXXV). But a few of these were made in parts, so that the rear disc could be, by a partial turn, slipped off from the shank, to facilitate insertion into the slits of the ear lobe. The front discs were rimmed with white shell rings, within which were narrower circlets of tortoise shell, and within these, in turn, little round, very dark and slightly protuberant wooden bosses or plugs, covered with gum or varnish and highly polished, so that the whole front of the button exactly resembled a huge round, gleaming eyeball. Indeed, this resemblance was so striking that both Mr. Sawyer and I independently recognized the likeness of these curious decorations to the glaring eyes of the tarpons, sharks, and other sea monsters of the surrounding waters ; and as the buttons were associated with more or less warlike paraphernalia, I hazarded the opinion that they were actually designed to represent the eyes of such monsters—to be worn as the fierce, destructive, searching and terrorizing eyes, the "Seeing Ears," so to say, of the warriors. This was indicated by the eye-like forms of many of the other ear buttons we found—some having been overlaid in front with highly polished concavo-convex white shell discs, perforated at the centres as if to represent eye pupils,—as in *f*, of the figure last referred to.

There were still other ear buttons, however, elaborately decorated with involuted figures, or circles divided equally by sinusoid lines, designs that were greatly favored by the ancient artists of these keys. The origin of these figures, both painted, as on the buttons—in contrasting

blue and white—and incised, as on discs, stamps, or the ends of handles, became perfectly evident to me as derived from the "navel
marks," or central involutes on the worked ends of univalvular shells ;
but probably here, as in the Orient, they had already acquired the significance of the human navel, and were thus mystic symbols of "the middle," to be worn by priestly Commanders of the warriors. That the ear
buttons proper were badges, was indicated by the finding of larger numbers of common ear plugs ; round, and slightly rounded also at either end,
but grooved or rather hollowed around the middles. Although beautifully fashioned, they had been finished with shark-tooth surface-hatch-
ing, in order to facilitate coating them with brilliant varnishes or pigments. The largest of them may have been used as stretchers for ordinary wear ; but the smaller and shorter of them were probably for ordinary use, or use by women, and had taken the place of like, but more
primitive ornaments made from the vertebræ of sharks. Indeed a few
of these earlier forms made of vertebræ, were actually found.

I could not quite determine what had been the use of certain
highly ornate flat wooden discs. They were too thin to have
been serviceable as ear plugs, or as labrets. But from the fact
that they were so exquisitely incised with rosettes, or elaborately
involuted, obliquely hatched designs, and other figures—the two
faces different in each case—and that they corresponded in size to
the ear buttons and plugs, I came to regard them as stamps used in
impressing the gum-like pigments with which so many of these ornaments had been quite thickly coated, as also, perhaps, in the ornamen-
tation or stamping of other articles and materials now decomposed. Very
long and beautifully finished, curved plates of shell had been used
probably as ear ornaments or spikes, also ; since they exactly resembled
those depicted as worn transversely thrust through the ears, in some of
Le Moyne's drawings, of which representations I had never previously
understood the nature ; and many of the plummet-shaped pendants I
have before referred to, must have been used after the manner remarked
on in some of the old writers, as *ear weights* or stretchers, and some,
being very long, not only thuswise, but also as ear spikes for wear after
the manner of using the plates just described. While certain crude examples of these curious pendants had been used apparently as wattling
bobbets, still others, better shaped, had as certainly served as dress or gir-
dle pendants. On one of them, made from fine gray coral stone—in form
like a minute, narrow-necked, pointed flask—the attachments were so
completely preserved that the delicate cords, intricately and decoratively interlaced to and fro from the groove cord surrounding the neatly
turned rim, to the central knot over its small flat head, were still perfectly
visible, the whole having been coated with shining black gum or varnish.
I may add, however, that some of the cruder and heavier of these shell,
coral, and coral-stone plummets, must have served purely practical ends.
Not a few had almost unquestionably been used, as I have said, as wat-

tling weights and netting bobbetts, their hurried finish, their adaptability to such uses and their numbers and the uniformity of many of them, all indicated this. Others, no doubt, had served as fish-line weights. Still, several of the more elaborate of them were not only decorated, but were so beautifully shaped and so highly polished that they could have been employed only as combined stretchers and ornaments or as insignia of a highly valued kind.

The remains of fringes and of elaborate tassels, made from finely spun cords of the cotton-tree down—dyed, in one case green, in another yellow—betokened high skill in such decorative employment of cordage. The remains, too, of what I regarded as bark head-dresses quite similar to those of Northwest Coast Indians, were found. Associated with these, as well as independently, were numbers of hairpins, some made of ivory, some of bone, to which beautiful, long flexible strips of polished tortoise shell—that, alas, I could not preserve in their entirety—had been attached. One pin had been carved at the upper end with the representation of a rattlesnake's tail, precisely like those of Cheyenne warriors; another, with a long conical knob grooved or hollowed for the attachment of plume cords. Collections of giant sea-crab claws, still mottled with the red, brown, orange, yellow and black colors of life, looked as though they had been used as fringe-rattles and -ornaments combined, for the decoration of kilts. At all events their resemblance to the pendants shown as attached to the loin-cloth of a man, in one of the early paintings of Florida Indians preserved in the British Museum, was perfect. Here and there, bunches of long, delicate, semi-translucent fish-spines indicated use either as necklaces or wristlets; but generally such collection were strung out in a way that led me to regard them as pike-, or shaft-barbs.

Certain delicate plates of pinna-shell, and others of tortoise-shell, square—though in some cases longer than broad—were pierced to facilitate attachment, and appeared to have been used as dress ornaments. Still other similar plates of these various materials, as well as smaller, shaped pieces of differing forms, seemed to have been inlaid, for they were worn only on one side, the outer, and a few retained traces of black gum on the backs or unworn sides.

Considerable collections or sets of somewhat more uniform tortoise-bone and pinna-shell plates, from an inch and a half to nearly three inches square, were found closely bunched together, in two or three separate places. None of them were perforated. Moreover, nearly all were worn smooth on both faces, and especially around the edges, as though by much handling. Hence it appeared that they had not been used as dress ornaments, or for inlaying or overlaying. One characteristic was noteworthy. In each collection, or set, which consisted of from twenty or more to forty or more pieces, a small proportion were distinguished from the others by difference in length or in material or in surface treatment. In one lot of between forty and fifty tortoise-bone plates, for example, there were four or five plates of pinna-shell, while on one of the tortoise-bone plates themselves were circularly incised the dolphin-like figures of two porpoises "wheeling" in the water—one above, the other below the medial suture of the bone, the line of which evidently represented the rippling surface of the water, for the figure above it was spiritedly depicted "blowing"—that is, with mouth open— the one below it, with mouth closed, as though holding the breath. Now from the fact that these differences were very marked in each set, and that many of the tortoise-bone plates of each, whether still covered with traces of the original epiderm or not, were so cut from the carapace at the intersections of the sutures, as to include portions of from one to six nearly equal-sized segments, I judged that possibly these *sets* of the plates, at least, had been used in sacred games, or perhaps in processes of divination—for abundant evidence that the tortoise and turtle were here—as in the Orient, and elsewhere in America,—held sacred, occurred with our finds in other parts of the court.

It will be observed that suggestions as to quite diverse uses of both the plummet-shaped objects and these plates, have been offered. In some cases these diverse uses of single types were perfectly manifest, but in others merely inferential. Let me repeat that there was frequently (and this was especially true of personal paraphernalia) evidence as to quite varied use of identical forms. It is always difficult to determine as specific, the purpose of a primitive art-form, for the high degree of differentiation characteristic of modern art was not developed generally in primitive art. It is particularly difficult to distinguish between the purely ceremonial and the more or less ornamental in such personal paraphernalia as I have been describing. To a certain extent all personal adornments, so called, of early peoples, are ceremonial or sacred, since the most rare and beautiful objects are like to be regarded by them as also the most effective charms or medicine potencies, if only because of their rarity, their substances and their colors.

As typical of primitive ornament proper I may mention the beads and pendants and certain of the gorgets of shell which we discovered. While it is true that even such objects were probably, as with other primitive peoples, supposed to be sacred,—for instance, on account of their substance and white color, because related by appearance to the shell-like white foam of the blue sea, and to the light or white splendor of day in the blue sky—the fact that they were found indiscriminately associated with other remains indicated equally indiscriminate use—use, that is, as ornaments more or less in our acceptation of the term. The commonness of the material of which they were made caused them to be prized less on account of their nature and beauty, than on account of the labor they represented. This is also indicated by the fact that their forms (wrought in species of shell here more common than elsewhere on the gulf coast), are nevertheless very widely distributed throughout other portions of Florida and all the Southern and Central Mississippi States;

a fact which argues that they, like the wampum of other regions, were used as the media of trade, or the basis of definite exchange valuation, as well as, in case of the more elaborate of them, in the solemnization of treaties. But by far the greater number of the articles of personal adornment described in preceding paragraphs, were more than this. They were found not indiscriminately, but definitely associated with other ceremonial remains. They may therefore be regarded as having been especially sacred, used as amulets, and in many cases, as at the same time badges of office, birthright, or priestly rank. Certainly this may be judged true of such as had been given distinctive forms, for semblance or form is to the primitive-minded man, the most significant character of any thing. The ear buttons already described illustrate this, as well as certain of the gorgets. These were about three inches in diameter, discoidal, and each cut out from the labrum of a pyrula or conch, to represent a broad circle enclosing a cross. Above the end of the upper arm of this cross, four holes were drilled (instead of one), for suspension. The margin of the inner side was, moreover, scored with definite numbers of notches. Thus it was plain that to the primitive nature worshipers who made and used such gorgets the circle represented the horizon surrounding the world and its four quarters—typified by the cross as well as the four holes or points—the notches in its rim, the score of sacred days in the four seasons pertaining to the four quarters thus symbolized; and that this kind of ornament, if we may still call it such, was the combined cosmical and calendaric badge, probably of the priest who officiated in, and kept tally of, the ceremonials, and ceremonial days, of the successive seasons.

Miscellaneous Ceremonial Appliances; Sacred and Symbolical Objects; Carvings and Paintings.

Less difficulty attended the determination of other than the strictly personal appliances of ceremonology which we found; and again, many articles of both these classes, the meaning of which might have been problematical had we found them dissociated, were readily enough recognized when found together. This was particularly the case with a heterogeneous collection of things I discovered close under the sea wall, at the extreme western edge of the court. I regarded its contents as having constituted the outfit of a "Medicine man," or Shamanistic priest. It is true that it contained several articles of a purely practical nature. There were two or three conch-shell bailers; one or two picks or battering tools of conch-shell, of a kind already described; and a hammer of a sort not infrequently found elsewhere. It was made from a large triton-shell by removing the labrum or two first larger whorls, from the columella, and leaving this to serve as the handle, while the remaining four or five smaller or apical whorls were left to serve as the head. There were also several hollow shaving-blades or rounding-planes, made from the serrate-edged dental plates or

mandibles of the logger-head turtle, and some shell chisels and cutters
of various other sorts.

For the rest, however, this curious assemblage of things both natural and artificial, were, judged by their unquestionable relationship
to one another, certainly sacred, or fetishistic. No other purpose could
be assigned to several natural but extremely irregular pearls; peculiarly shaped, minute pebbles and concretions ; water-worn fragments of
coral exhibiting singular markings, such as regular lines of star-like or
radiate dots; more than twenty distinct species of small, univalvular
shells, and half as many of small bivalves—all quite as fresh as though
but recently gathered. These were mingled with oliva-shell buttons
and pendants, and pairs of sun-shells (solenidæ), two of which had been
externally coated with a bright yellow pigment, and others of which
had once been painted, inside, with symbolic figures or devices in black,
although the lines of these figures could now no longer be distinctly
traced. There were a number of interesting remains of terrestrial animals. One was the skull of an opossum. It had been carefully cleaned,
and cut off at the occiput, and to the base thus formed, the under jaw had
been attached frontwardly at right angles, in such manner that the
object could be set upright. The whole had been covered with thick,
white pigment, and on this background lines in black, representative of
the face marks or features of the living animal, as conventionally
conceived, had been painted, doubtless to make it fetishistically "alive
and potent" again. Another skull, that of the marten or weasel,
occurred in this little museum of a primitive scientist; and since we
know that both the opossum and the weasel were favorite "mystery
animals" of Indian Shamans elsewhere, little doubt remains as to the
character of the collection they belonged to. But there were other more
artificial objects, yet of a kindred kind. There were kilt-rattles, made
from peculiarly mottled claw shells of both the small sea-crab and the
great king-crab ; and a set of brilliant colored scallop shells, and
another set of larger pecten shells, all in each set perforated, obviously
for mounting together on a hoop, to serve as castanets, precisely as are
similar shells among the Shamans of the far-away Northwest coast.
There was still another kind of rattle—duplicated elsewhere—made
from the entire shell or carapace of a "gopher," or land-tortoise, the
dorsal portion of which was very regularly and neatly drilled, to aid
the emission of sound. As though to show us that the original owner
of this collection was not only a sacred song-man and soothsayer or
prophet, but also a doctor, there were, in addition, a beautiful little
sucking tube made from the wing-bone of a pelican or crane, and near
at hand a sharp scarifying lancet of fish bone set in a little wooden
handle, of precisely the kind described by old writers as used by the
Southern Indians in blood letting and ceremonial skin-scratching.

In addition to these and other objects largely of natural, or of only
partially artificial origin, there were a number of highly artificial things.

Most interesting of these and conclusively significant of the nature of the find, was what I regarded as a set of "Black-Drink" appliances. It consisted of a gourd, the long stem of which had been perforated at the end and sides; of a tall wooden cup or vase—brewing-churn and drinking-drum, in one; of a toasting tray of black earthenware punctured around the rim to facilitate handling when hot, and of a fragmentary, but nearly complete, sooty boiling-bowl or hemispherical fire-pot, also of black earthenware. Near by were two beautifully finished conch-shell ladles or drinking cups, both rather smaller and more highly finished than others found in different parts of the court. The larger one was still stained a deep reddish brown color inside, as though it had been long used for some dark fluid like coffee, and uncleansed, or too deeply stained for cleansing.

Now by reference to Laudonnier's relation of Ribault's and his own efforts to colonize Florida, some three hundred years ago, and especially by reference to Jonathan Dickenson's narrative of his reception by the self-same "Cassekey"—who, it will be remembered, later despoiled him and his party—one can see that these things quite undoubtedly pertained, as I have intimated, to the brewing and ceremonial serving of the sacred Cassine or ' Black-Drink" so famous among all Southern Indians; for they correspond in a general way quite remarkably to those described by this author, so much so, that I do not hesitate to quote his account at length. He says :

"The Indians were seated as aforesaid, the Cassekey at the upper end of them, and the range of cabins was filled with men, women and children, beholding us. At length we heard a woman or two cry, according to their manner, and that very sorrowfully . . . . which occasioned some of us to think that something extraordinary was to be done to us; we also heard a strange sort of a noise, which was not unlike the noise made by a man, but we could not understand what, nor where it was; for sometimes it sounded to be in one part of the house, sometimes in another, to which we had an ear. And indeed our ears and eyes could perceive or hear nothing but what was strange and dismal, and death seemed to surround us; but time discovered this noise to us—the occasion of it was thus : In one part of this house, where a fire was kept, was an Indian man, having a pot on the fire, wherein he was making a drink of a shrub (which we understood afterwards by the Spaniards, is called Casseena) boiling the said leaves, after they had parched them in a pot; then with a gourd, having a long neck, and at the top of it a small hole, which the top of one's finger could cover, and at the side of it a round hole of two inches diameter. They take the liquor out of the pot, and put it into a deep round bowl, which being almost filled, contains nigh three gallons; with this gourd they brew the liquor, and make it froth very much; it looks of a deep brown color. In the brewing of this liquor was this noise made, which we thought strange; for the pressing of the gourd gently down into the liquor, and the air which it contained, being forced out of the little hole at the top, occasioned a sound, and according to the time and motion given, would be various. This drink when made and cool to sup, was in a shell first carried to the Cassekey, who threw part of it on the ground, and the rest he drank up, and then would make a loud hem ; and afterwards the cup passed to the rest of the Cassekey's associates, as aforesaid ; but no other man, woman or child must touch or taste of this sort of drink ; of which they sat sipping, chattering, and smoking tobacco, or some other herb instead thereof, for the most part of the day.''

A much fuller account of this solemn ceremonial, of the making and administering of the "Black-Drink," as well as of its meaning at almost every stage, is given in the admirable annals of William Bartram—a former and honored member of this Society—whose works are, indeed, the source of more definite information regarding the Southern Indians than those of any other one of our earlier authorities on the natives of northerly Florida and contiguous States.

Three other objects in the curious lot of sacerdotal things I have been describing were especially typical ; for closely related, but varied forms of them were found at several other points throughout the area we excavated. One was a small, square, paddle-like tablet, about six inches long, three inches wide, and five-eighths of an inch thick. At one end, presumably the lower, was a sort of tenon ; that is, the board was squarely cut in from either side to the middle, where a projection about an inch wide and a little more than an inch long was left, as though either for insertion into a mortice, or to facilitate attachment to something else, otherwise. A much larger tablet or board, an inch thick and six or seven inches wide, by nearly two feet in length, also tenoned in like manner at the lower end, lay on edge near by. Along the middle of one face of this tablet, two elongated figures were cleanly cut in or outlined, end to end, figures that seemed to represent shafts with round terminal knobs—indicated by circles—the sides of the shafts being slightly incurved, so that the figures as a whole greatly resembled the conventional delineations of thigh bones as seen in the art-works of other primitive peoples—in, for example, the codices, and on the monuments, of Central America. Another tablet of this sort, somewhat wider, longer, and more carefully finished by the shaving down of its surfaces with shark-tooth blades, showed likewise along the middle of one face similar devices, carved, however, in relief, as though to represent a pair of thigh bones laid lengthwise and end to end upon, or rather, set into the centre of one side of the board.

Near the first described of these curious objects which I regarded as probably mortuary, was another tablet, evidently of related character ; but it was much more elaborate. The lower portion was tenoned and in general outline otherwise resembled the tablets I have described ; but above this portion, midway from end to end, it was squarely notched in at either side, and above the stem thus formed, extended, in turn, a shovel-shaped head, or nose, so to call it, as may be better perceived by reference to Fig. 2, Pl. XXXIV, which represents the most perfect of these objects that we found. The specimen in question was between three and four feet long, although less than a foot in width. The lower portion was not more than an inch in thickness, and was uniformly flat, the upper portion—head or nose, as I have called it—was convex on one side, flat on the other. When I found this object I encountered the somewhat rounded shovel-shaped end first, and thought that I had found a paddle. Following it up by feeling with my fingers along the edges, I became assured that this was so, when I struck the notched-in portions at the stem which connected it with the lower or flatter and squarer portion. Then when the shoulders of this in turn were touched, I supposed it to be a double sort of paddle. I discovered my mistake only when the entire object was revealed. These curious tablets, tenoned at the lower ends, notched in midway, and terminating in long shovel-shaped extensions beyond the necks thus formed, were represented by no fewer than ten or twelve examples besides the one described. They were found quite generally distributed throughout the court. But they varied in size from a foot in length by three inches in width, to nearly five feet in length, by more than a foot in width. The most elaborate of them all was the one already referred to, and shown in Pl. XXXIV, for it, like the first specimen found, had been decorated with paint (as at one time probably had been all of the others). Upon the head or shovel-shaped portion were two eye-like circles surrounding central dots. At the extreme end was a rectangular line enclosing lesser marginal lines, as though to represent conventionally a mouth enclosing nostrils or teeth or other details. The body or lower and flatter portion was painted from the shoulders downward toward the tail-like tenon with a double-lined triangular figure, and there were three broad transverse black bands leading out from this toward either edge. On the obverse or flat under surface of the tablet were painted equidistantly, in a line, four black circles enclosing white centres, exactly corresponding to other figures of the sort found on various objects in the collections, and from their connection, regarded by me as word-signs, or symbols of the four regions.

That these curious tablets were symbolical—even if designed for attachment to other more utilitarian things—was indicated by the fact that various similar objects, too small for use otherwise than as batons or amulets, were found. Several of these were of wood, but one of them was of fine-grained stone (Fig. 3, Pl. XXXIV), and all were exquisitely finished. Those of wood were not more than eight inches in length by three inches in width; and they were most elaborately decorated by incised circles or lenticular designs on the upper convex sides— still more clearly representing eyes—and by zigzag lines around the upper margins as clearly representing mouths, teeth, etc., and on the same side of the lower portions or bodies, by either triangular or concentric circular figures; while on the obverse or flat side of one of them was beautifully incised and painted the figure of a Wheeling Dolphin or Porpoise, one of the most perfect drawings in the collection. The little object in stone (disproportionately illustrated in Fig. 3, Pl. XXXIV) was only two inches in length by a little more than an inch in width. It was wrought from very fine dioritic stone, and as may be seen by the illustration was so decorated with incised lines as to generally resemble the comparatively gigantic wooden object of the same general kind shown above it. The very slight tenon-like projection at the lower end of it was, however, grooved, as if for attachment by a cord. Plainly, therefore, it was designed for suspension, and no doubt constituted an amulet representative of the larger kind of object. The moderately small, highly finished wooden figures of this kind, seemed also to have been used more as portable paraphernalia—as batons or badges in dramatic or dance ceremonials perhaps—than for permanent setting up or attachment. That this may have been the case was indicated by the finding of a "head-tablet" of the kind. It was fifteen inches in length by about eight inches in width, although wider at the somewhat rounded top than at the bottom. On the flatter, or what I have called the under side of the lower portion or end, this tablet was hollowed to exactly fit the forehead, or back of the head, while on the more convex side, it was figured by means of painted lines, almost precisely as were the upper surfaces of the small wooden batons or minature carved tablets. My conclusion relative to its character as a "head-tablet" was based, not only upon the fact that it was thus hollowed as though to fit the head, but also upon the comparison of its general outlines and those represented on its painted surface, with the outlines and delineations on certain objects represented on the head-dresses of human figures etched on shell gorgets found in the ancient mounds of the Mississippi Valley.

I admit that the significance of not only the smaller, but also of the larger of these remarkable tablets must remain more or less enigmatical ; yet, judged by their general resemblance to the gable-ornaments upon the sacred houses and the houses of the dead of various Polynesian peoples, and to corresponding sheet-copper objects of the northwest coast, as well as to their obvious connection with the tablets found by us, on which conventional representations of thigh bones occurred, I was led to believe that at least all of the larger of them were ancestral emblems ; that the smaller and more highly finished of them were, therefore, for ceremonial use, perhaps, in dramatic dances of the ancestry, in which also such head-tablets as the one I have described were used ; and that such amulets as the little one of stone here figured, were likewise similarly representative. It may be, however, that while there is no question as to the symbolic and ceremonial nature of all these things—as is indicated by the like conventional devices upon them all,—nevertheless, the larger of them may have been used in other ways ; as, for example, on the prows of canoes, or at the ends of small mortuary structures—chests or the like—or they may have been set up to form portions of altars. But in any one of these uses they might well have served quite such a symbolic purpose as I have suggested ; for they were obviously more or less animistic and totemic, and it is for this reason that I have provisionally named the larger of them "Ancestral Tablets," and look upon the smaller of them as having been used either as amulets or to otherwise represent such tablets in the paraphernalia of sacred ancestral ceremonials. I may add that I believe it will yet be possible, by the experimental reproduction and use of these forms, to determine more definitely what the originals, the most mysterious of our finds, were designed for.

In addition to the head tablet I have spoken of, various thin, painted slats of wood were found in two or three places. They were so related to one another in each case, that it was evident they had also formed portions of ceremonial head-dresses, for they had been arranged fan-wise as shown by cordage, traces of which could still be seen at their bases. Besides these, other slats and parts of other kinds of head-dresses, bark tassels, wands—one in the form of a beautifully shaped spear, and others in the form of staffs—were found ; many of them plainly indicating the practice of mimetically reproducing useful forms, and especially weapons, for ceremonial appliance.

Perhaps the most significant object of a sacred or ceremonial nature, however, was a thin board of yellowish wood, a little more than sixteen inches in length, by eight and a half inches in width, which I found standing slantingly upward near the central western shell-bench (Section 22). On slowly removing the peaty muck from its surface, I discovered that an elaborate figure of a crested bird was painted upon one side of it, in black, white, and blue pigments, as outlined in Fig. 1, Pl. XXXIV. Although conventionally treated, this figure was at once recognizable as representing either the jay or the king-fisher, or perhaps a mythologic bird-being designed to typify both. There were certain nice touches of an especially symbolic nature in portions of this pictorial figure (and the same may also be said of various other figures illustrated in the plates), the nicety of which is not sufficiently shown in the drawings, that were unfortunately made from very imperfect prints of our photographs. It will be observed, however, not only that considerable knowledge of perspective was possessed by the primitive artist who made this painting, but also that he attempted to show the deific character of the bird he here represented by placing upon the broad black paint-band beneath his talons (probably symbolic of a key), the characteristic animal of the keys, the raccoon ; by placing the symbol or insignia of his dominion over the water—in form of a double-bladed paddle—upright under his dextral wing ; and to show his dominion over the four quarters of the sea and island world thus typified, by placing the four circles or word-signs, as if issuing from his mouth,—for in the original, a fine line connects this series of circlets with his throat, and is further continued downward from his mouth toward the heart,—as is so often the case with similar representations of mythologic beings in the art of correspondingly developed primitive peoples.

On exhibiting this painting to that learned student of American linguistics, Dr. Albert S. Gatchet, of the Bureau of American Ethnology, and stating to him that I regarded it as that of the crested jay, or of the king-fisher, he called my attention to the fact that among the Maskokian tribes of Georgia, and of contiguous southern regions, the name of a leader among the recognized warriors signified "He of the Rising Crest," and that this name was also that of the jay whose crest is seen to rise when he is wrathful or fighting. I am therefore convinced that this figure, so often found in the south and in other parts of Florida (and usually identified as that of the ivory-billed woodpecker), really represented the bird-god of war of these ancient people of the keys, his dominion over the water being signified, as I have suggested, by his double-bladed paddle ; his dominion over the four quarters of the world, by the four word-signs represented as falling from his open mouth—for these circular signs, as we have seen before, were not only drilled in the margin of gorgets symbolic of the four quarters, but were also inscribed upon some of the tablets I have called "Ancestral."

Other, smaller, thin painted boards were found, but it was evident that they were lids or other portions of boxes,—some of which, indeed, we found nearly complete. One of these lids was not more than seven inches in length, by four inches in width. Upon one side of it was drawn, in even, fine lines of black (as approximately shown in Fig. 6, Pl. XXXIV), the representation of a horned crocodile. Again, in this as in the painted tablet, may be seen a clear indication of a knowledge of perspective in drawing, on the part of the primitive artists who designed it. This is apparent in the treatment of the legs, of the serrated tail, and of the vanishing scales both at the back and under the belly of the figure. Such knowledge of *delinative art in the round*—remarkable with a people so primitive—was, I believe, derived by them from their still more remarkable facility in relief work, in wood carving ; and this, in turn, originated, I think, in their possession of those admirable carving-tools of shark teeth that I have previously described The little lid in question was found still in connection with the ends and with one side of a jewel-box, in which had been placed several precious things, among them, two sets of ear buttons and choice, carved wooden and shell discs. It was enfolded within decayed matting containing a bundle or pack, in which were also nine ceremonial adzes, a pair of painted shells, a knife with animistically carved handle, and other articles—all evidently sacred, or for use in the making of sacred objects. The little figure of the crocodile painted on this lid, was of interest in another way. Being horned, it at once called to mind the "horned alligators," described by Bartram and others, as painted upon the great public buildings of the Creeks or Maskokian Indians of the States just north of Florida. Upon another box-lid or tablet was painted in outline, a graceful and realistic figure of a doe, and along the middles of the ingeniously rabbetted sides and ends of these boxes—whether large or small—were invariably painted double lines, represented as tied with figure-of-eight knots, midway, or else fastened with clasps of oliva shell—as though to mythically join these parts of the boxes and secure their contents.

The painted shells I have referred to as contained in the pack just described, were those of a species of Solenidæ, or the radiatingly banded bivalves that are locally known in that portion of Florida as "sun-shells." Each pair of them was closed and neatly wrapped about with strips of palmetto leaves that were still green in color, but which of course immediately decomposed on exposure to the air. On opening this pair of them, I found that in one of the lids or valves, the left one, was a bold, conventional painting, in black lines, of an outspread hand. The central creases of the palm were represented as descending divergingly from between the first and middle fingers, to the base. This was also characteristic of the hands in another much more elaborately painted shell of the kind, that was found by Mr. George Gause within four or five feet of the bird-painting or altar-tablet. As may be seen by reference to Fig. 4, Pl. XXXIV, this painting represented a man, nearly nude, with outspread hands, masked (as indicated by the pointed, mouthless face), and wearing a head-dress consisting of a frontlet with four radiating lines—presumably symbolic of the four quarters—represented thereon, and with three banded plumes or hair-pins divergingly standing up from it. The palm-lines in the open hands of this figure were drawn in precisely the same manner as were those in the hand painting of the pair of shells found with the ceremonial pack, and the thumbs were similarly crooked down. Upon the wrists, and also just below the knees, were reticulate lines, evidently designed to represent plaited wristlets and leg-bands. Otherwise, as I have said, the figure was nude. It was not until our excavations were well advanced beyond the middle sections of the court of the pile dwellers, that these singular painted shells were discovered, since they were closed when found as were those in the collections that I found under the sea wall at the southwestern margin of the court. Throughout the richer portions of the court which we had already passed over, we had quite generally encountered these closed sun-shells, so many of them, in fact, that we had usually thrown them aside; since we had regarded them as intrusive, as probably the remains of living species that had found their way into the court after its abandonment. Hence I have no doubt that we missed many treasures of this kind of symbolic painting From the small number of specimens we recovered, it is difficult to surmise what could have been the purpose of these painted shells. There is of course no doubt that they were ceremonial or sacred, but whether they were used in Shamanistic processes of divination or not, it is measurably certain that they were regarded as potent fetiches or amulets, for in the one that contained the painting of the outspread hand that I myself found and opened, a substance, which I regarded as decayed seaweed, had apparently been placed to symbolize, in connection with the figurative hand, creative potency; for algæ and the green slime of the sea is regarded by many primitive peoples as earth-seed or world-substance. Unfortunately I did not see the other shell until after it had been opened by Messrs. Gause and Bergmann; but hearing their cheers over the discovery, I ran immediately to the spot, and had the good fortune to rescue it before attempt had been made to wash it out. For although, as has since been ascertained, the paint employed in its delineation was made from a quite permanent, gummy substance (probably rubber), yet when first found it was almost fluid, like that on many others of the paintings.

When I exhibited this specimen and the drawing of the open hand to Mr. Clarence Moore, whose interest in these finds has been from first to last so gratifying, he kindly called my attention to a concavo-convex or shell-like plaque of stone, found in a mound in southern Illinois, in which an almost identical figure of an open hand was incised. In a shell disc discovered in Georgia, there is, I have also recently learned, an etched delineation of an open hand containing an eye-like figure ; and I am therefore the more inclined to regard the sort of shell paintings we found as not only in a high degree symbolic and sacred, but also as typical, and I also incline to believe that they were, moreover, the earlier forms of the etched or graven figures of the kind just described as found in the more northerly mounds.

As evidenced by the exquisite finish and ornamental designs of so many of the implements weapons and utensils I have described, the ancient key dwellers excelled especially in the art of wood-carving. While their arts in painting were also of an unusually highly developed character,—as the work of a primitive people—their artistic ability in relief-work was preëminently so. This was further illustrated in a lit tle wooden doll, representing a round-faced woman wearing a sort of cloak or square tunic, that was found near the southernmost shell-bench along the western side of the court, in Section 15. Near this little figure was a superbly carved and finished statuette in dark-colored, close-grained wood, of a mountain-lion or panther-god—an outline sketch of which is given in Fig. 1, Pl. XXXV. Nothing thus far found in America so vividly calls to mind the best art of the ancient Egyptians or Assyrians, as does this little statuette of the Lion-God, in which it was evidently intended to represent a manlike being in the guise of a panther. Although it is barely six inches in height, its dignity of pose may fairly be termed "heroic," and its conventional lines are to the last degree masterly. While the head and features—ears, eyes, nostrils and mouth— are most realistically treated, it is observable that not only the legs and feet, but also even the paws, which rest so stoutly upon the thighs or knees of the sitting or squatting figure, are cut off, unfinished ; bereft, as it were, of their talons. And this, I would note, is quite in accordance with the spirit of primitive sacerdotal art generally—in which it was ever sought to fashion the form of a God or Powerful Being in such wise that while its aspect or spirit might be startlingly shown forth, the powers associated with its living form might be so far curtailed, by the in-completion of some of its more harmful or destructive members, as to render its use for the ceremonial incarnation of the God at times, safe, no matter what his mood might chance, at such times, to be.

60

MASKS AND FIGUREHEADS.

To me, the remains that were most significant of all discovered by us in the depths of the muck, were the carved and painted wooden masks and animal figureheads. The masks were exceptionally well modeled, usually in realistic representation of human features, and were life-size; hollowed to fit the face, and provided at either side, both above and below, with string-holes for attachment thereto. Some of them were also bored at intervals along the top, for the insertion of feathers or other ornaments, and others were accompanied by thick, gleaming white conch-shell eyes (as in Fig. 2, Pl. XXXIII) that could be inserted or removed at will, and which were concave—like the hollowed and polished eye-pupils in the carving of the mountain-lion god—to increase their gleam. Of these masks we found fourteen or fifteen fairly well-preserved specimens, besides numerous others which were so decayed that, although not lost to study, they could not be recovered. The animal figureheads, as I have called them, were somewhat smaller than the heads of the creatures they represented. Nearly all of them were formed in parts; that is, the head and face of each was carved from a single block; while the ears and other accessory parts, and, in case of the representation of birds, the wings, were formed from separate pieces. Among these animal figureheads were those of the snouted leather-back turtle, the alligator, the pelican, the fish-hawk and the owl; the wolf, the wild-cat, the bear and the deer. But curiously enough, the human masks and these animal figureheads were associated in the finds, and by a study of the conventional decorations or painted designs upon them, they were found to be also very closely related symbolically, as though for use together in dramaturgic dances or ceremonials. On one or two occasions I found the masks and figureheads actually bunched, just as they would have been had they thus pertained to a single ceremonial and had been put away when not in use, tied or suspended together. In case of the animal figureheads the movable parts, such as the ears, wings, legs, etc., had in some instances been laid beside the representations of the faces and heads and wrapped up with them. We found two of these figureheads—those of the wolf and deer—thus carefully wrapped in bark matting, but we could neither preserve this wrapping, nor the strips of palmetto leaves or flags that formed an inner swathing around them. The occurrence of these animal figureheads in juxtaposition to the human masks which had so evidently been used ceremonially in connection with them, was most fortunate; for it enabled me to recognize, in several instances, the true meaning of the *face-paint* designs on the human masks thus associated with these animal figures. I cannot attempt to fully describe the entire series, but must content myself with reference only to a few of the more typical of them.

Near the northernmost shell bench, in Section 20 of the plan shown on Pl. XXXI, was found, carefully bundled up, as I have said, the remarkable figurehead of a wolf with the jaws distended, separate ears, and conventional, flat, scroll-shaped shoulder- or leg-pieces, designed for attachment thereto with cordage, as shown in Fig. 1, Pl. XXXIII. A short distance from this specimen was found the beautifully featured man-mask sketched in Fig. 2 of the same plate. Now both of these specimens had been painted with black, white, and blue designs, which unfortunately cannot be shown with sufficient clearness in the uncolored sketches. When I observed that the designs on the human mask represented, albeit conventionally, the general features and lines of the wolf figurehead associated with it, I was no longer at loss to understand the connection of the two. It will be observed that on the ear-pieces of the wolf figurehead, are two well-defined and sharp-pointed dark areas representing the openings of the erect ears, and that correspondingly, above the eyebrows of the mask itself, similarly pointed black areas are painted, while the tusked open mouth of the wolf figurehead is also represented by jagged, or zigzag lines on the mask, extending across the cheeks upward to the corners of the mouth, apparently to symbolize the gnashing teeth of the wolf; and even the conventionally represented shoulders and feet of the springing wolf figurehead are drawn in clean white lines over the entire middle of the face of this mask. It was therefore evident to me, that these painted lines upon the human mask were designed, really, to represent the aspect and features and even the characteristic action or spring, of the wolf. Hence I looked upon these two painted carvings as having been used in a dramaturgic- or dance-ceremonial of these ancient people, in which it was sought to symbolize successively the different aspects or incarnations of the same animal-god, namely the wolf-god, —that is, his animal aspect, and his human aspect.

Now this association of the animal figureheads with the masks presenting their human counterparts was not exceptional. In another portion of the court the rather diminutive but exquisitely carved head, breast and shoulders (with separate parts representative of the outspread wings, near by) of a pelican, was found, and in connection with this, a full-sized human mask of wood, also. Upon the forehead, cheeks, and lower portion of the face of this mask, was painted in white over the general black background, the full outline (observed from above) of a flying pelican, as may be better seen than imagined by a comparison of Figs. 3 and 4, in Pl. XXXIII—especially if I explain that the under lip and chin of this man-pelican mask was quaintly pouted and protruded to represent the pouch of the pelican—in a manner that does not show in the full-face drawing.

The remarkable and elaborately carved and painted figurehead of the leather-back turtle; the large figurehead or mask-like carving representative of a bear—its face also elaborately painted—and others of the animal figureheads which we found, were likewise paired or associated with their human presentmentations or counterparts—that is, human masks painted with practically the same face-designs as occurred on these animal figures.

The symbolic unity, or general similarity of painted designs on the masks with human features to the face paintings or markings on the very realistic animal figureheads grouped or associated with them, gave me a new insight into the meaning of mask painting in general, and into the meaning also of even simple face painting as practiced so widely among primitive peoples, especially among such as use masks in their dances or other sacred and dramatic ceremonials. That the interpretations I shall presently venture to offer may seem less far-fetched than otherwise they might seem, I will explain a little more fully, the tendency peoples of this kind have, toward reproducing, in their face-paintings or upon their masks, the characteristic marks or features of animal faces. I cannot better do this than by making a few statements regarding the philosophy of form I was taught whilst living with some very primitive-minded people—the Zuñi Indians—some years ago. Since they observe that life is never manifest save in some sort of *form*, they argue that no form is without some sort of *life*, and since they further observe that each particular kind of life is manifest in some particular kind of form, they argue that form strictly conditions life—its powers and other characteristics. Naturally, therefore, they accord to forms (or rather to semblances) even of inanimate things, such potencies as they see manifested in the forms of the animate beings these things most resemble externally or otherwise. Let me illustrate this. They connect the wave-, or ripple-like scales of fishes with their ability to live and float in the wave-fretted waters ; they believe it is chiefly because of the cloud-like down under or between the feathers of a soaring bird that he is able so lightly to fly among the similar, fluffy or downy clouds—for these of themselves like the mist of living breath, ever float without effort. To such a people, of course, form, semblance, aspect, is therefore all important ; and they naturally think that by reproducing a given form or appearance which of itself gives rise to a certain effect, they may again and unerringly produce, or help to reproduce the same effect, with the form of their own making.

This sort of reasoning about analogy between form and function, between creatures and the phenomena that resemble their operations, between animals and things, is only touched upon here—just sufficiently to indicate how a people thus reasoning further reason that as the lives, conditions and powers of animals differ as do their forms, so the specific traits or characters of animals differ according as do their differing aspects, especially according as do the expressions of their countenances ; and finally, that since the facial expression of each kind of animal is unvarying in all members of the species, and the corresponding trait or character of each is equally unvarying, they reason that expression controls, rather than that it is the result of, character or disposition—so far at least as these animals are concerned. It follows that they believe the changes in the expression of a man's face to be similarly effective. They observe that his face is far more mobile than is that of any animal, and hence believe that he is more capable of changing ; that according as his mood changes, his face changes ; and they reason that *vice versa* according as his face is changed his mood must necessarily change.   Further, they believe that not only according as his face changes so does his mood change, but also that his traits or his entire character may, for the time being be changed, by *wholly* altering, with paint or other marking, with mask or other disguise, the entire expression of his countenance or aspect.   Just as a wrathful warrior, with glaring eye and drawn mouth, and alert or defiant attitude, resembles to some extent a mountain lion or a panther at bay, so by the painting upon his face and upon other portions of his person of the characteristic markings of the panther, he may be made to assume still more fully the nature of the panther.

Now when we reflect that the peoples who reason thus are also in a totemic phase of development sociologically—largely because they do reason thus—that they are inclined, each according to his tutelary deity or the totem of his clan, to emulate the animal (or supposedly living plant or thing) that is his clan totem, in both behavior and appearance so far as possible—in order to become so far as possible incarnated with his spirit—we find one of the many reasons he has for painting his face with the aspect, or face marks, of some special animal.   Moreover, in this reasoning may be found a primal explanation for his supposition that by putting on a mask he can more utterly change for the time being ; can even change his totem or relationship ; can become, to quote from the Zuñis, " That which he thirsts to become," or " Desirously needs to become, what tho' a God," strictly according to the expression (and name) or aspect, of the mask he makes and marks and puts on. Thereby, it is believed that so far as he resembles in facial aspect or expression one kind of being or animal or another kind of being or animal, he will become that being or animal, or at least, be possessed by its spirit.

Nothing short of a full treatise on this primitive philosophy of analogy, and the relation thereto of maskology or disguise by costuming, painting, tattooing, bodily distortion or mutilation and the like, as a means of becoming actually incarnated with the spirits of ancestors, mythic beings, and animals, or totem gods, would fully explain the significance of the bunched animal figureheads and animistically painted human masks that we found.   I may add, however, that one can see how far reaching was this primitive conception of the life-potency of form, or expression, by examining any sorts of ancient vessels that are decorated with maskoids or diminutive representations of human or semihuman countenances.   Almost always these maskoids — whether found on mound-builder vessel, Central American jar, ancient Peruvian vase, or even Etruscan urn—are characteristic, according to the style of expression they represent, of some particular kind or use of the vessel they occur on.   They have often, indeed, been described as grotesques, caricatures and the like, usually without any further explanation ; yet the absence of a humorous conception or intent in their portrayal is demonstrated by the fact that if we study the relation of the primitive vessels on which they occur to other things, with which, for example, they are sometimes found, we shall speedily discover that each curious mask upon such vessel is but the exaggerated expression of a character or being it was sought to associate in some way—as by fixing its potency—with the "being" and purpose, of the pot itself, and this is especially true of vessels designed for ceremonial use.

A strikingly perfect example of the kind of animal carving I have earlier characterized, was the figurehead of a deer, which Gause and I found near the edge of the northernmost of the shell benches along the western border of the court (in Sec. 22, Pl. XXXI). It was lying, in a very natural position, on its side. Thus seen in the midst of the dark muck, its light-hued painted lines vividly revealed by contrast, its large, deep brown eyes wide open and lifelike—for the pupils were formed of polished, cleverly inserted discs of tortoise shell—it was the most winsome and beautiful figure of the head or face of a doe or deer that I have ever seen, albeit so conventionally treated. The illustration of this figurehead shown in No. 2 of Plate XXXV, by no means does justice to the graceful lines of the original carving, or to the fineness of the painted decorations thereon, for the view is too directly full-faced. The earpieces had been attached to the back of the head by means of cords passing over pegs thrust through them and then through bifurcated holes at the points of attachment to the head-piece, in such manner that they could be used as pulleys for the realistic working of these parts; and the unpainted edge, as well as peg-holes all around the rearward portion of the head, plainly indicated that the skin of a deer or some flexible substitute therefor, had been also attached to it, the more perfectly to disguise the actor who no doubt endeavored in this disguise to personate the character of the deer-god or dawn-god, the primal incarnation of which this figure was evidently designed to represent.

A mask of purely human form was also found not far away. It had evidently been associated with the figurehead in such ceremonials as I have referred to. At any rate, like the figurehead itself, it had over the eyebrows a crescent-shaped mark—which seems, by the way, to have been the forehead-symbol of all sorts of game-animals amongst these people, as betokened by its presence on the forehead of the rabbit carving and of other similar animal carvings. It also had the tapered, sharp-pointed white marks or patches along either side of the nose above the nostrils, observable on the snout of the deer head, and the four sets of three lines radiatingly painted around the eyes to represent winkers. This latter characteristic in the eye-painting of the deer figurehead, is very noteworthy; for it would seem that it was intended to symbolize, by means of the four sets of three lines, not merely the eyelashes of the deer, but also rays, of the "eye of day" or the sun. This I infer the more unhesitatingly because, according to the accounts given by more than one early writer on Florida, the deer must have been regarded among some of the Floridian tribes as one of the gods of day or of the dawn—as indeed is both the antelope and the deer among the Zuñis. In such event they symbolized—just as do similar sets of radiating lines around paintings of the Zuñi sun-god—the four sets of the sun's rays that are supposed to correspond to the four quarters of the world, as well as to the four sets of three months in the corresponding four seasons of the year over which the sun god is believed to have dominion—since he creates all the days thereof.

Not only were the human masks associated with their animal counterparts, but sometimes two or more of the human masks were found in one such group. In two or three instances we found multiple sets of them. In such case they were superimposed, as though they had been tied or wrapped, one inside of the other, and thus hung up or laid away, and had fallen so gently into the water-court that their relation to one another had not been disturbed thereby. A notable example of this kind was found in the association of two masks—one lying directly over the other, the faces of both turned upward—that lay not far away from the turtle-figurehead that I have already described. The painted lines on the lowermost of these masks were indicative that it was designed to represent the man-turtle or man-turtle god; whilst the lines upon the superimposed mask seemed, from their general resemblance to the face marks painted upon the bear-figurehead I have also described, to indicate that they were designed to represent the same sort of human presentmentation of the bear. I am at loss to account for this singular consociation of the two masks—the turtle-man mask and the bear-man mask—unless by supposing that the ancient people who made them, regarded the somewhat sluggish turtle as the "bear of the sea," and the bear, whose movements are also awkward, as one of his "brother-turtles of the land," or that they otherwise mythically related them.

We found several human masks by themselves. One was clearly, from the length of its sharp nose and the painted lines upon its features, designed to represent the cormorant; another, from the oblique or twisted form of its mouth, its nose awry, and its spiral or twisted face-marks or bands, as plainly represented the sun-fish or some other slant-faced fish. I regarded a third one of these masks as that of the man-bat-god. It was of especial interest, not only on account of its associations, but also on account of its general resemblance to the face of the bat-god of night conventionally depicted so frequently on Central American monuments. Still another mask was of equal interest, for it represented unmistakably, in a half-human, half-animal style, the features of the wild-cat; and the curiously doubled paint lines with which its cheeks were streaked downwardly below the eyes, although strictly regular and conventional, were singularly suggestive of the actual face-markings of the wild-cat, and thus enable us to understand the significance of like lines that are incised upon certain purely human-faced figures characteristic of many of the maskoidal pipes from mounds of the Ohio and Mississippi valleys.

I would once more call attention to the association in *groups* or *sets*, of the animal figureheads and especially of the masks, as affording still further proof of similarity, if not identity, in key-dweller art and mound-builder art, and as thus affording also a satisfactory explanation of certain points observable in delineations I have so often heretofore referred to as occurring upon the shell gorgets and copper-plates of the ancient mounds of Georgia and other Southern States. Almost always, in these delineations of the mythic human figure, it may be observed that while upon the face, a mask is plainly portrayed, yet, in one or other of the hands is as distinctly represented another mask—not a head, as has frequently been supposed,—and I am therefore inclined to believe that, as with the key dwellers, so with these peoples of the mounds, dramas representative of the transformation of gods from animal into human form, and from one human character into another human character, were probably attempted in their sacred dances.

Such a figure of the mound plates as I have described is shown in No. 3, Pl. XXXV, of the accompanying illustrations. It is drawn from one of the celebrated copper-plates of the "Etowah Mound" of Georgia, and I have reproduced it here (from one of Prof. William H. Holme's superb drawings) not only to illustrate this statement regarding the probable ceremonology of duplicated masks in both cases, but also to illustrate various other points of close similarity between the art remains of the two peoples. The so-called baton, held in the right hand of the figure in this plate, may be seen to correspond very closely to the war-club which we discovered in the court of the pile dwellers, and which is outlined in front thereof ("a," of the same figure). It may be seen, too, that the winged god here portrayed wears not only a beaked mask, but also a necklace of oval beads, and an elongated pendant depending therefrom, like those we so frequently found; an ear button, also exactly like those we found (shown in "d" of the same figure); that around the wrists, arms and legs of this primitive portrait are represented reticulate or plaited bands, as around the wrists and legs of the figure painted in the sacred shell I have described ("b" and "c"); and that finally, this character bears in his left hand a mask, the face lines and ear plug of which as closely resemble those that we actually found (as shown in "e" and "f" of the figure) in the court of the pile dwellers.

GENERAL CONCLUSIONS.

In reference to the general significance of these observations and finds in southwestern Florida, I must necessarily be brief, since this paper has already reached a length that was not, when I began, contemplated.

As to the origin of the key-dweller phase of existence, it was, I think, so much influenced by certain coastal conditions, that a few words on the physiography of the Lower Gulf section of Florida which best exemplifies them, will not be amiss.

The whole coast, even from as far north as Tarpon Springs to the extreme end of the Peninsula, is low and sandy ; the highest natural land rarely rising more than a few feet above high-tide level, and the loftiest dunes nowhere reaching an altitude of over fifty feet. Geologically, Florida, Prof. W J McGee tells me, is an extension of the lowland zone—made up of later mezozoic and cenozoic deposits—fringing our Atlantic and Gulf coasts, and, as one of your Secretaries, Dr. Persifor Frazer, also states, reappearing in several of the Antillean islands. Especially do the prevailing formations of Florida resemble those of the Peninsula of Yucatan. They are of very pervious limestone, and from above the region of Charlotte Harbor southwardly, are interspersed with phosphatic beds, also of organic origin. But whether indurated, as are the lowermost, or less solid as are the more superficial, these formations are, like the overlying soil, excessively sandy. Hence they are not only pervious, but also, very soluble in the acids of fresh surface- or rain-water. One of the consequences of this is, that areas of varying extent and in lines generally parallel with the courses of the open rivers and inlets of the country, and of their tributaries, are subject to undermining by these corrosive processes ; have fallen in, forming first deep lakes, then, as these in time have become filled, morasses, in the central lagoons of which, through the peculiar habits of alligators and other aquatic creatures, circular mud-banks have been thrown up, becoming cypress islets, and, finally, the foundations of hammocks, or marsh-keys like those of the Anclote region—built there by man in later ages. Everywhere, too, along the lines of narrower subterranean rivers formed by more restricted dissolving away of the underlying formations, series of perfectly round, hopper-shaped sinks occur, seemingly fathomless, containing pellucid or deep green water, and reminding one measurably, not only of the round, artificial drainage basins of the keys, but also of the more natural (and in some ways identical) çenotes or ancient well-caves of Yucatan and other portions of Central America.

Not to enter as fully as I ought into a discussion of the physiography of this inner portion of the coast—so suited to settlement by a people like the key dwellers, when they came inland—I may say that the conditions described render the whole region peculiarly unstable. This has been especially true of the actual coast. Everywhere it is indented by such tidal inlets as the Manatee and Pease, or their sluggish inland extensions called rivers, like those of Anclote, and those that put out from the north and east of Charlotte Harbor, and those which everywhere radiate sinuously in the same general directions, from the great indentation or bay that contains the Ten Thousand Islands. In a land so broken and low as this, the hurricane has wrought continuous change of shore-line, and 'tis but natural, too, that its coast should be skirted by wide reefs, paralleled by long-reaching, sea-enclosing, narrow, tide- and wind-heaped sand-islands such as already described ; and that all its hither shores should be nearly tide-low, traversed by forbidding marshes, and fringed by almost impenetrable swamps of cypress and mangroves. Even the mouths of its creeks, rivers and inlets, are shift- ing and treacherous, and are also filled with shoals, almost if not quite exposed, at low tide. As a consequence, approach, even in light craft, is —save in special places sundered by many miles of unnavigable shal- lows—wellnigh impossible. I regard this feature as having had a pre- ponderating influence in causing the ancient key dwellers—whether they were derived from the mainland or whether, as I have reason to think, they were alien comers to these shores from some distant region over the sea,—to locate as they did, out in the midst of the open waters.

Again, no waters in the world so teem with food-producing animals —mollusks, fishes, crustacea and turtles—as do these waters of the lower Florida Gulf-coast. Yet to a people dwelling inland—save in such favored, far-sundered sections of the country as I have mentioned— this abundance would be all but valueless, in consequence of the diffi- culty of shoreland navigation. What more natural, then, than, as I have endeavored to picture in earlier chapters of this paper, that these peo- ples should have followed the example of the pelican and cormorant, and located their stations for food-winning, and finally their dwelling- places themselves, out in the midst of the navigable, but still not too deep, shoreland seas ? That they did so, ages and ages ago, is unques- tionable. That the structures which they reared, more or less modified, in many cases, the further distribution of shoals, sand reefs, tidal swamps and the lowlier of the fringing islands themselves, is also un- questionable—as I might proceed to show by entering into a discussion of the results of my investigations of certain of the keys that, although once free islets, are now connected with the capes of the outer islands ; and of certain others that have, in fact, been almost buried in sand-drift, as was the Ellis Settlement. But suffice it if I say that not only have wide stretches of sandy shoals drifted up between all the humanly con- structed reefs of the olden time that lie near the land—especially those to the south—but also, that wide mangrove swamps have grown up around them, as among the Ten Thousand Islands, evidencing the vast antiquity of the earliest key-building and key-builders here.

There are, however, other evidences of great antiquity, more directly of interest to us as anthropologists. One of these evidences is manifest in the character of the art displayed on all of the more finished objects we found in the keys ; for this was of a highly, and at the same time dis- tinctively conventional kind. Now I scarcely need state of primitive art- forms, that wherever they have obviously originated and have become highly conventionalized in, and yet are still recognizably characteristic of, a peculiar region—to the degree to which those of this art were characteristic of the environment we found them in, they are the product of a *very* slow growth. Certainly, while this art of the keys may not have been, nay, was not, altogether of a strictly local origin, it was in the main, of a kind which one might expect to find developing or developed in such an environment. Everywhere, for example, evidence of the influence of shell, shark-tooth, and other sea-produced materials—used as implements in the working of wood, bone and horn, and of shell itself—could, as I have shown, be traced here ; and had plainly, as I have also shown, given rise to special ornaments on particular parts of things thus made. But the point of interest is, that these ornaments were not only conventional, but that they had already become conventionally *specialized ;* were, many of them, indeed, so highly conventionalized and thus so specialized, that except for the completeness of our series, they could not have been traced to their simple, incidental origin in the kinds of tools used, modes of working employed, and materials worked. I have said that this kind of conventionalization in art and localization of decorations, is of exceedingly slow growth. This is because genera-tions, if not ages, are required for the radical modification of a single specialized ornament on any particular part of a specialized tool or implement, weapon or ceremonial appliance, among primitive peoples ; owing to such peculiar conceptions of the meaning and potency of form as I have already discussed in its relation to ceremonial objects, and will presently again refer to as particularly relating to things practically used. By way of a single example, I may instance the circular obvolute, or navel ornament (as I have called it), in its relation to the ends of the hard-wood handles of certain classes of tools in the collection. I have referred to this as having been derived directly from the double spiral or obvo-lute observable on the cut-off apices or ends of conch- or busycon-shells and other univalvular shells. I have also suggested that the use of kingfish jaws and shark-tooth knives in girdling sticks, by a process of cutting around and around the sticks always in the same direction, with-these sharp, yet jagged tools, produced, as shown by many specimens in the collection, rough, spiral rosettes at the ends of the sticks. Now when the sticks were severed in the same way, but first from one side then the other, the figures produced at the ends of them strikingly resembled the involuted spirals at the ends of the worked shells. Thus, although the figure when associated with purely ceremonial objects doubtless signified the "navel" or "middle"—as earlier suggested—yet it came to be associated also with the ends of the handles of tools the working parts of which were made of the columellæ of shells on the ends of which it naturally occurred. Thus, for mythic reasons, the figure was doubtless considered not only appropriate, but even essential to the handle, no less than to the shell armature of such a tool, in order to harmonize its parts, to give potency or effectiveness to it as a whole. So too, with the radiate or rosette figures found on the ends of very small handles made from saplings. It was observed that when suitable saplings were cut off squarely and sufficiently smoothed, little check-lines, such as one may see on the sawed-off end of a seasoned stick, always appeared, radiating from the heart toward, but not quite to, the circumference of the severed segment. Thus the figure came to be exaggerated decoratively, and associated with the end of another special kind of working tool and, for like mythic reasons, was retained. The steps by which these originally half-natural or accidental markings became developed as decorations, then localized on special tool-handles, and then so characteristic of special types of tools as to be laboriously reproduced even in other material than wood—like the horn and bone sometimes substituted therefor—could only have been taken very slowly.

Still more confidently may this be affirmed of the art displayed on objects less evidently of local origin, for they illustrated an equally slow and much longer continued process in the development of conventional art, that of survival—as on the box-tablets described; which, being no longer held together with double cords or strands lashed around them and tied over their middles with square- or reef-knots (double figure of eight knots) had come to be secured with gum and pegs, yet must still be mythically tied with *painted* strands and knots in imitation of the "good old way." In this connection I would again refer to the superb celt-handle, the decorations on which were so very highly conventionalized and so modified by the introduction of shell-volute figures and of certain eye-marks derived from knots (the one kind of figure being generic on the shell tool handles just referred to, the other on the crooked adze handles, as shown in Fig. 2, Plate XXXII), that it was with difficulty the main lines and bands on the shaft and head could be recognized at all, as survivals of the wrappings or bindings on simpler and earlier forms of this kind of instrument.

If these forms of decorations on tools, and their association with special parts thereof—whether of extraneous or of autochonous origin, possessed as they were, of so high a degree of conventionalization—were of great age in development, this must to a much greater extent have been the case with the yet higher degree of conventionalization shown in the representation of face and body marks on animal carvings and paintings in the collection. In the first place, these marks on, for instance, the faces of the figureheads, were not irregular, as they are seen to be on the faces of the natural animals they represented. While the forms of these figureheads were realistic to a degree, the painted or incised face marks were remarkably conventional, regular, and almost perfectly symmetrical. That is, stripes were represented as clean bands, patches or spots as neat circles or figures, sometimes elaborated into highly ornate curved devices. Yet as a whole, these painted or incised face markings were so distributed and contrasted as to look startlingly natural when seen at a distance. To give an idea of the great degree of conventionalization thus attested, I have only to state that this kind of highly artificial and ornate representation of the face markings of animals betokens an attempt on the part of the primitive artist to represent the *ideals*, the perfect ancestral types or spiritual archetypes, of the animals portrayed—for it is supposed, as is told in the numberless beast-tales of his people, that the present animals, descendants of these great and perfect ancestors, have been changed by their own deeds, their disobedience of the gods, their strifes and what not, and that thus their countenances are distorted or besmirched, and fixed so in token of their rashness or misfortunes in creation time. So this kind of conventionalization represents myth, as well as art ; both, developing and interacting uninterruptedly throughout a very long period of progress in a given organic environment. If this be true of the *style* of the art, it is doubly true of its *symbolic specialization*. For it has been seen that in case of the figures of timid creatures—game-animals, like the figurehead of the deer, the carvings of the rabbit and other creatures of the kind—all were characterized by a crescent-shaped device on their foreheads. Thus, this conventional mark was not merely that of an individual representative of the species, but it was, so to say, a generic mark, representative of several species of the same general kind. This is further shown by the fact that another special kind of marking was equally characteristic of animals of prey—of the wildcat, the panther, the bear and their kind. In the carvings of each one of these fierce creatures, the outlines of the eyes were not only sharply pointed in front but in each case terminated behind in three sharp triangular lines or marks pointing backwardly, and giving to the face of the animal figure a peculiarly crafty, yet sinister look. That this too was a generic mark, is still further indicated by the fact that it occurred also upon one of the human masks corresponding to the figurehead of one of these fierce creatures. Now in this generic kind of marking we have not only a still higher art development, but also a very much higher mythic development betokened, since it indicates that these ancient peoples regarded the game-animals as of one great family or descent, and the prey-animals as of another great class or lienage, and that they were thus, in a way, naturalists of no mean order.

The interest of the significance of this particular sign of the eye as pertaining to or symbolizing prey-beings, is enhanced greatly by the further fact that upon many of the exquisitely finished and highly conventionalized carvings of the heads of these kinds of beasts (and of the faces of warriors or men wearing masks animistically corresponding to them as well) that are found so frequently in the mounds of the Mississippi Valley, of Tennessee and even of Ohio, precisely the same conventional marking or barbing of the eye—as though it were set in the figure of a stemmed and barbed arrow-point to make it " piercing "—is observable. Thus, through a study of the conventional treatment of such figures here in the keys of lower Florida, we not only arrive at an understanding of a new meaning of these figures or lines around the eyes of maskoids and head-carvings found in the far away north (namely, that they represent animals of prey or their human counterparts), but we also see that the same art was, in these widely separated regions, so identical in this particular, that we cannot but assign to it a single cultural origin. That is, we must look upon it as having originated in one or the other, the northern or the southern portion of the area throughout which it was so generally distributed; as having spread from that single centre in the one or the other direction. Now the bulk of evidence at hand favors the belief that the place of origin of the peculiarities I have noted, was here in the far south; probably, among the keys.

Be this for the moment as it may, the enormous distance to which these characteristic art forms had spread after long-continued and full development, must have required a still more enormous length of time. This is a further and a much more impressive indication of the very great antiquity of the art in question. For the spread of special art forms in definite relation to particular implements or figures is, among primitive peoples, not so frequent or facile as is usually supposed; and when in rare cases it does occur, it is effected with exceeding slowness. We may account for the spread of arts among primitive peoples in two ways; first, by barter and intercourse, conquest and adoption; or, second, by actual derivation or descent, that is, by actual spreading to a greater or lesser extent, of the people among whom the art prevails and originated. While we may hold that, in the wide diffusion of arts common alike to the keys and the mounds, both of these causes acted to some extent, still, if we consider a little further the way in which arts spread among primitive peoples—why slowly—we can, I think, arrive at a more definite understanding of the question as to which of the two causes above stated was the more active, and as to whether the art traveled from the Gulf northward, or from the north southward. First, then, the mere fact that early peoples attribute to distinctive forms particular existences and potencies, indicates that one people would be slow to adopt unchanged from another, an unaccustomed form, even of so simple a thing as an implement, and especially as a weapon or a ceremonial object; since the unaccustomed form of the first would be supposed by them to render it inefficient; of the second, unsafe; and of the third, diabolical; while all would be held to be unsuited, because unrelated to themselves. It must be constantly borne in mind that these ancient theorists believed their implements and weapons and amulets to be alive, and felt that the powers of these things were not only strengthened, but were also restricted to or rendered safe for, special uses, as well as made to be related to their *makers*, by their forms or by the decorations or figures placed upon them, especially when these were highly symbolic. It is for this reason more than any other, that primitive peoples cling so to forms, and are so chary of borrowing new forms of implements or weapons, etc. When they do borrow the fashions of such things, they proceed at once to cover or invest them with the peculiar decorative or symbolic devices that they are accustomed to associate with the same kinds of things in time-honored use among themselves. It is chiefly due to this tendency that we have kept inviolate for us everywhere in the primitive world, signs on the relics we find, of what have been termed cultural areas or areas of art-character-ization. And so, while the extensive and long-continued intercourse in the barter of the far-southern peoples of Florida and the keys, with more northern peoples (which is so positively indicated by the occur-rence in the northern mounds, of gorgets, etc.—not only derived from species found nowhere else than in these Gulf regions, but also treated in precisely the same conventional manner), will account for much in this spread of identical art forms, nevertheless it does not, I am inclined to think, explain the whole. To say for the moment nothing further of the great variety of art forms which almost certainly took their origin in the region of the keys or in some other Gulf region where a life of similar kind was naturally or necessarily followed, and which are also found throughout the mound area, I may call attention to a single point among many—the evidence afforded by the tempering-material of pottery. Almost always, the pottery of sea-dwelling peoples, in regions where clays of such kind as require tempering occur, is tempered with calcined and crushed shell. In an article on "The Germ of Shoreland Pottery" (printed in the *Memoirs of the International Congress of Anthropology*, pp. 217–234, Chicago, The Schulte Publishing Com-pany, 1894), I have endeavored to show why this is so, and was at first naturally, if not inevitably so. Now, wherever the art forms I am dis-cussing are found in the mounds, even at far inland points, the potteries of these same mounds are commonly tempered with shell, notwithstand-ing the fact that in the more inland and northerly regions of the mounds such kind of tempering had to be supplied, at great labor, from fresh-water species of mollusks.

There are, however, various additional reasons, it seems to me, for sup-posing that this art spread northwardly from a southern sea-environment —not so much by barter, as by actual movement landwardly and north-wardly, of the culture and to some extent of the peoples themselves of these southern sea-land regions. One of these reasons rests in the very broad distinction that we may make between the sea-shell art of the mounds and the sea-shell art of other and more northerly regions, equally as far inland from the sea. There, objects made from sea shells are abun-dant, it is true, but they are in general, obviously of a more purely decora-tive or valuative, than of a symbolic character. This was the case, for example, with the famous wampum of New England and the Middle Atlantic States, prized for the high value of the far-derived material of which it was made, more than for its supposed sacred or ancestral quali-ties; whereas, the greater number of the shell cups, gorgets, and other shell articles found in the mound region proper, retained the identical pristine symbolic character and association they naturally had on the seashore. Now it is not easy to see how this could have been the case had the peoples of the mounds originated, or rather had their culture, customs and art originated, in the northern or inland region, and proceeded thence to the sea.

I would again mention the wide prevalence in the keys, of the distinctively conventional treatment of carved and incised work,—whether on shell, bone, or stone,—illustrated by so many specimens in our collection, in connection with its almost equally wide prevalence on figures found in the mounds ; which art-vogue was, it would seem, more at home in the keys—more in accordance with a seaside environment that appears to have originated these conventional forms and modes of treatment—than in the lands of the north. The identity of costume represented, too, in the case of the painted shell as compared with incised shell gorgets and embossed copper-plates of Tennessee and Georgia, is obvious, as may be seen by reference to the single illustration herewith furnished in Pl. XXXV, Fig. 3.

It is significant that the forms, as well as the surface decorations of the potteries which we found somewhat inland, in the more northerly region of Tarpon Springs and of the Anclote (and this applies also to shoreland-like examples of pottery that I have seen from the still further interior and more northerly portions of Florida, and even from western Georgia) were in many ways distinctively and indisputably derived from precisely such gourd- and woodenware and shell-shaped vessels and utensils as we found in the keys. It was thus obviously the pottery of a people who had been accustomed to use gourd-shells and wood, more than clay, for the making of their vessels, and not only so, but to use wooden vessels that had been made with cutting implements of shark-teeth and shell. This was clearly evidenced in the hachured surfaces of so many of the vessels ; in the reticulated surfaces of others of them—which represented the end grainings of wood—and in the fine, convoluted or concentric, stamped or incised designs obviously derived from curly-grained wood or paddles made thereof, which characterized the surface decoration of so much more of this pottery. When we add to this the fact that here in the North and in the interior, the points of many blades of flint were made not only in the usual lanceolate or leaf-shaped form, but also in the asymmetrical form of shark's teeth, and that now and then even exquisitely polished stone adzes were formed as obviously in imitation of naturally curved shell adzes—such as were constantly found in the keys—it is perfectly evident that the peoples who built up, in the marshlands here, the hammocks, and built near them the little lake-encircled mounds, were originally a people of the sea, not of the mainland, were a people who had once lived as the key dwellers-lived, on island mounds in the sea or its shoals, here using such implements as their ancestors had there used, and carrying ancestral ideas of habitation and of utensils down from generation to generation, and so, slowly up into the land.

The theory I have ventured to advance heretofore, in regard to the relation of key building in the sea to mound building on the land strongly supports the evidence just adduced as afforded by the correspondence of these potteries and other art remains from mounds in the North, to the art types of the keys in the South. No other theory of the origin of mound building in general, thus far advanced, especially of mound building as it was practiced in the Mississippi and Ohio regions and all through the Southern States, accounts, it seems to me, so satisfactorily or so directly and simply, for the origin of this remarkable practice. We have seen how, for many reasons, it was necessary for the key dwellers to build their mound-like homes or islands, out in the seas. Thus were they near their chief source of food supply ; thus were they freed from the almost insupportable pest of mosquitoes and other insects of the sub-tropic marshy mainland ;* thus were they safe from any human enemies they might chance to have ; and building as they did, special mounds upon these shell islands of theirs for the foundation of special kinds of structures—temples, storehouses or public buildings, places of resort in danger—they were not only protected from the terrific hurricanes and tidal waves that sometimes swept the Gulf seas, but also, I conceive, they developed the habit of erecting great mounds for special structures of this kind to such extent, that it became fixed ; so customary traditionally, that whithersoever they or rather their descendants went thereafter, they continued the practice as an essential tribal regulation. At least we find evidence enough in nearly all the old historic records from the Sixteenth to the Eighteenth century, that generally the Southern Indians (especially the Maskokean Indians and Nachez) were still building mounds of precisely this kind, that is, for the temples of their Priests and for the dwellings and assembly places of their Mikos, "Suns" or King-like Chieftains. Again, along with the development of key and mound building for the living, in the sea, and later in tide marshes or lowlands, we have seen that there was also developed, through ancestralism, the habit of building somewhat similar places for the tribal dead. This also was practiced in the interior, as shown by prehistoric monuments ; by the early tribes of the Southern States, as equally indicated by

* Soon after my return from Florida, last spring, Dr. O. T. Mason, of the United States National Museum, kindly called my attention to the following passage, on page 291 of *The History of the Caribby Islands*, rendered into English by John Davides, in 1666, from an earlier work by Rochefort. I quote it here in full, as it so unexpectedly confirmed my previous inference relative to the only really important influence of the mosquito as a factor in human progress, that I have ever learned of. Speaking of the Caribbeans, he says :

"Their habitations are somewhat near one to another, and disposed at certain distances, after the manner of a village ; and for the most part they plant themselves upon some little ascent, that so they may have better air and secure themselves against those pestilent flies, which we have elsewhere called *Mesquitos* and *Maringoins*, which are extremely troublesome, and whereof the stinging is dangerous in those parts where there is but little wind stirring. The same reason it is that obliges the *Floridians*, beyond the Bay of Carlos and Tortugnes, to lodge themselves for the most part at the entrance of the sea, in huts built on piles or pillars."

I would add that the last clause is especially significant in connection with our discoveries in the "Courts of the Pile Dwellers."—F. H. C.

narratives of the first explorers. Thus, especially throughout the mound-building area—primarily in the lowlands of the Mississippi and tributary rivers, then on higher land along these, and finally on the terraces, and even the plateaus of rivers in the still farther north—we find almost always these two kinds of mounds associated ; that is, so-called "Temple" and "Domicilary" mounds, and the tumulæ of the dead or "Burial mounds ;" and I believe that wherever these two kinds of mounds are found thus associated (as they were naturally and necessarily associated in the keys, and as we have seen that they were associated historically in the Southern States) the evidence is that they were the works of peoples who were either themselves derived from the southern sea islands, or who derived thence their culture, and, if so, a portion at least, of their ancestral population.

Observable facts in regard to mound building of this kind the world over, support this theory of its origin in *sea environments*. Since the subject is so important, I may enlarge upon it by calling attention to the fact that everywhere, the principal builders of mounds, barrows and tumulæ, have ever been maritime peoples, or at least peoples living along great rivers of the sea. Such were the heroic seafaring Greeks of Homer's time, the roving Vikings of Scandinavia. In fact everywhere —and this applies especially in countries famed for the size and extent of their prehistoric shell heaps—the story is much the same ; that old peoples of the sea seem ever to have sought to lift themselves or their dead above the tide and flood ; to build, as it were, islands even on high land, wheresoever, in the course of ages, they happen to have here and there penetrated into the interior, or else to build foundations like to the refuse heaps of their ancestry, for the priests and other revered personages among their living.

As bearing intimately upon this question in its relation to such ancient remains of our own land, and particularly to the earlier historic Indians of the Southern States (who, as I have said before, were builders of mounds for the support of their public structures), I may here refer to the remarkable statements contained in some of the early writings, regarding others of their characteristics.

It has been seen again and again, that surrounding all the ancient keys, were shell-bank enclosures approached by canals that had, presumably, been used as fish-pounds or -preserves. It goes far toward establishing my theory of the derivation from the key dwellers, or from peoples living practically their life, of some at least of these Southern mound-building peoples, when we read in the narrative of the expedition dition of Don Hernando de Soto amongst these same peoples (1539–1541), presented by the Knight of Elvas to the Spanish King and Council of the Indies, that " On Wednesday, the nineteenth day of June, the Governor entered Pacaha, and took quarters in the town where the Cacique was accustomed to reside. It was enclosed and very large. In the towers and the palisade were many loopholes. There was much dry maize, and the new was in great quantity throughout the fields. At the distance of half a league to a league off were large towns, all of them surrounded with stockades. Where the Governor stayed was a great lake near to the enclosure, and the water entered a ditch that wellnigh went round the town. From the River Grande to the lake was a canal, through which the fish came into it, and where the chief kept them for his eating and pastime. With nets that were found in the place, as many were taken as need required ; and however much might be the casting there were never any lack of them.''

Now since the very origin of key building was directly related, in all probability, to the improving of natural, then the making of artificial bayous to serve as fish-pounds ; to the building of fishing stations near by, and resultantly, to the construction of shell settlements in place thereof, we cannot reasonably suppose that the key builders derived all this from the mainland, but rather that the dwellers in the interior here spoken of by an eye-witness, had derived their practice of making such fish canals and preserves, from them or from ancestors like them.*

If, then, the key-dweller and Southern seashore and flood-land phase of life and art was, as is here indicated, the originative, the earlier phase, and the mound-builder phase was the later or to some extent inherited phase, it does not follow that the mound builders acquired their art and culture from the *particular* key dwellers the remains of

---

* To state my opinion clearly in reference to this question of the relation of the mound builders to the particular key builders the remains of whom we investigated, I may say that I do not believe this relation to have been necessarily direct, however much it may seem to have been so. The remarkable correspondence in the art characteristics of the mound remains proper, when compared with those exhibited in objects of our collections from the keys of the farther south, signifies to my mind, primarily, that the art displayed in objects from the inland mounds was inherited or derived from key-dwelling or sea-dwelling methods of technique and art treatment. This (leaving out all other questions) is indicated by numerous examples of mound art. I need mention only two or three. One is exemplified in the double-bladed battle-axe type of war club, figured in Pl. XXXV (3, a). The club of this type that we discovered at Marco was wholly of wood, yet it was evidently, as I have hitherto stated, a survival of the double, semi-circularly bladed war-axe of an earlier time. But it was, nevertheless, a practical, not merely a ceremonial, weapon. Now such a weapon is represented on the embossed copper plates and is engraved repeatedly on the shell gorgets of the mounds, as held in the hands of purely *ceremonial* figures. It is also sometimes found represented (among mound-remains, but not among those of the keys) in the shape of small amulets wrought of shell or stone. Again, a single nearly full-sized specimen, made wholly of stone, rather than of wood, (it is beautifully fashioned from light colored flint by chipping and battering, then grinding and polishing) has been very recently secured, I understand, by that fine authority on mound archæology, General Gates P. Thruston, President of the Tennessee Historical Society of Nashville, Tenn. All of these mound forms of the weapon, however, are strictly ceremonial : that is to say they are not directly *originative* forms, but forms of the weapon inherited and ancestrally venerated, that is, *derived* from some older form still adapted to *practical* use—as was the specimen we recovered from Marco. The same may be said of the shapely carving in green-stone, of a nearly full-sized, hafted celt—found in a sepulchral mound in the Cumberland Valley near Nashville, Tenn., some years since, by Prof. Joseph Jones—the correspondence of which as a type form, to the *actual* celt, found by us at Key Marco, is almost exact, save in merely decorative details of the handle.

whom we investigated. It is simply an indication, I think, that they derived it from like sea-dwelling people—very probably related to such key dwellers, and who possibly had their home farther up the Gulf. Not only are there at present other keys extending, interruptedly, from Tampa to the northwestern extremity of Florida, but between that point and the Delta of the Mississippi is also another very considerable group of islets which I regard as keys—judged by their distribution on the map. Whether they are actual shell keys, or not, remains to be determined. But the formations of the lower Mississippi are late Quaternary. Thus, in comparatively recent times, geologically speaking, we may assume that the area they cover was a northwardly extension of the Gulf, and that for ages later, conditions like those presented by the southern marshy shorelands into which the key dwellers seem to have ultimately penetrated must have prevailed, even unto comparatively recent times, anthropologically or historically speaking. The coast farther down was shoal, and fringed with islets—some, possibly, artificial. Thus the whole region was still suited to such modes of life as I have referred to, even well on toward modern times. And so, from this point of view, the Gulf shore and its border lands to the north and the northeast, no less than farther down, seems to have been as much an *area of characterization* as that of the keys we examined certainly was—of the southern and farther northern mound-builder culture. Therefore my claim is, that the best and most primitive, that is, originative illustration of this that we have, is to be found in these key-dweller remains. I must not be understood, however, as claiming that the moundbuilder phase of culture pertained *wholly* to descendants of the key dwellers or even of sea peoples like them. Cultures belong less, primarily, to distinct peoples than to distinct environments. An environment and the essential conditions of human existence therein, makes indeed, not only a culture, but goes far toward making a race; that is, toward moulding or unifying, racial traits, in whatever kind of man or kinds of men come into it and there remain for a sufficient length of time.*

I believe the relationship of the key dwellers to other Southern Indians and to the more ancient mound builders, both in the South and in the farther North, may, however, be regarded, as indicating more than merely parallel development; that this relationship may be considered as having been actual, and accultural, as well as primarily environmental; for the whole region of the mounds, which generally corresponded to the great flood-plain regions of the Mississippi and its mighty tributaries—and in this was not unlike the shorelands of the Gulf—

---

* If one but glimpse at the natives of like low sea-lands, of let us say, Borneo, Papua, Southeastern Asia and certain Polynesian regions, he will see how close a parallelism in arts—and probably, too, even in institutions and religion—obtains between the key dwellers as indicated by their art remains, and these peoples not in any wise related to them. He will see that merely by a similar condition of natural surroundings, these parallelisms have been wrought to a point that is, in many details of the products of these wide-sundered peoples, no less than astounding.

possessed throughout, also, much else in common, particularly in the matter of biotic characteristics, plant and animal life as they prevailed in at least the marshy borders and immediately contiguous lands. Such characteristics, since so intimately associated with subsistence and art activities, are of course the most potent of factors in giving direction to the movements and developments of primitive peoples,—especially when combined with generally like physical conditions throughout a given area,—and go far in themselves toward making thus, a distinctively *ethnic* area. Let me offer an example of this : In its way, the arid region of our farther Southwest, is more distinctive than is the region of the Southern seas and great contiguous rivers and flood-plains. That is, it is a region the climatic conditions of which are so homogeneous and so pronounced throughout, and the flora and fauna of which are therefore so uniform, that it has been potent to mould into or toward a common condition and type, and a common state of mind, too, nearly all the peoples who have ever entered it and therein dwelt long enough. In the centuries of a far-off time, it presently made of little bands wandering and seeking refuge in its desolate wastes—seeking throughout them for water and seeds—petty agriculturists. It forced them as they throve apace, to permanent occupancy, then to cultivation of, these far-sundered watering-places ; then, later, through contentions over these places and possessions, with other comers or with one another, to occupancy of and building in the cliffs, for defense. Thus out of such hard conditions was born the famous Cliff Dweller, his architecture, and his culture. It was my good fortune, years ago, to first definitely relate the Zuñi Pueblo Indians, linguistically and traditionally, with these ancient denizens of the cliffs, and to ascertain positively, and announce in various publications (especially of the Bureau of Ethnology) that the architecture of these and other Pueblo Indians was almost wholly, as they were themselves in part, derived from that of older cliff dwellers. But it seems that the Northerly cliff dwellers were the first in this long succession, as the Zuñis were (to the extent to which they were descended from them) their earliest successors. Yet as the ancestors of other Pueblo peoples penetrated into that constraining region, they too, under the potent influence of the same environment—probably more than by the example of these earlier predecessors who had been wrought upon thereby—adopted, one after another, a precisely similar mode of living and building. It is only eight or nine hundred years since the Navajo and Apache Indians gradually descended from their far-northern homes into this desert region. The Navajo Indians are not Pueblos, but it is sufficiently evident from facts relating to them given in the splendid treatises of Dr. Washington Matthews, that they were, especially along the line of their sociologic and religious development and the art thereto pertaining, rapidly becoming moulded, by accultural and environmental conditions combined, to the Pueblo condition of mind and life ; and had their course of development thus, not been cut short by the coming of the Spaniard with his present to them of flocks and herds that made nomads of them again, these already half-settled peoples would have become more settled and would have gone on developing precisely as older populations had there developed, the more rapidly because acquiring liberally from these older populations. Thus in the course of a similar period, or perhaps even in less time, they would no doubt have become Pueblos among the Pueblos.

Now I cannot but look upon the mound-building phase of life as, like the Pueblo-building phase, something that was influenced in a similar manner; and so, while I have no doubt that the ancient mound builders represented, as do the various modern Pueblos, several distinct *stocks* of men, still I believe that all owed their culture and their mound-building proclivities to the original common influence of sea-shore or key-builder life, and that each successive wave of peoples who penetrated the mound area from elsewhere, acquired the practice by the combined influences of the area to much of which it was so eminently suited, and of the peoples who had therein already become fixed in it.

In like manner as the art of the mound builders seems to have been related to that of the key builders, so certain forms found by us in the keys appeared, as heretofore intimated, to have been inherited from, or directly affiliated to, that of the farther south—of the Antilles, and even of South America. I need only refer to the labret and ear button, the latter of which, although common enough in the mounds, was still more prevalent in the keys, and was a peculiarly southern object of adornment, having prevailed universally throughout northern South America, and, indeed, throughout meridian America generally. This is true also of both forms of the atlatl found by us. They were not only South American as well as Central American in type, but on them were repeated even the decorative details of Yucatecan forms. In the pointed and spooned paddle; in the celt which, with its counterpart in stone from the Cumberland (and in little amulets from other portions of the mound area) which corresponded strictly with celts found throughout the greater and lesser Antilles; and finally, in the remarkable war club I have described in a former page, this affiliation of art-types was even more strikingly apparent. For, as I would repeat anew, this form of war club, at least, could scarcely have been other than a survival of a double, semicircular bladed hatchet that is peculiarly a South American type, as were war clubs like it—and also derived from it—in both South and in some portions of Central America.

When it is reflected that a not inconsiderable number of other forms found by us in the court of the pile dwellers were, as were those that I have so particularly referred to, almost too minutely identical with like southern forms to admit of wholly independent origin (although there is every probability that they had developed, even if elsewhere, yet in a generally similar kind of environment), and when this fact is considered in connection with the trend from south northwardly past the keys, of the main current of the Caribbean sea (as shown in Pl. XXV) and with the usual course of the great but intermittent Gulf hurricanes, it seems to me highly probable that not from the mainland, but from the sea, not from the north, but from the far south, the primitive or earliest key dwellers, whoever they were, came or were wafted in the beginning. While it is true that only a few years after the discovery by Columbus, the earliest voyagers to the Gulf of Maracaibo found peoples living there (as some few of them still live) in pile-supported houses out in the midst of the shallow waters, and hence named the country Venezuela or "Little Venice," and while it is also true that this current of the Caribbean Sea thence takes up and is thence reinforced by the current of the mighty Orinoco, still I do not believe that the derivation of these foreign arts of the key dwellers, or of the key dwellers themselves, may be traced quite so directly as that. I believe, rather, that here and there all through the waters washing the shores of lands southward from Florida—of Cuba, of Yucatan, of northern South America—we shall shortly find, unless the maps deceive me, evidence of a former very wide distribution in that direction of the key-dweller phase of life, and it has seemed to me that as the key dwellers of Florida may have borrowed from these older and more widely distributed peoples of their kind (who were probably more of South American than of North American extraction) so other peoples along that lengthy way, may also probably have derived many of their characteristics, and some small proportion of their populations perhaps. A study, for instance, of the ruined cities of Yucatan and some other portions of Central America, makes it clear that although the Mayas and other peoples who built them had advanced to a remarkable stage of barbaric civilization, and were possessed of a very highly developed architecture, yet they were at most, only highly, advantageously developed and elaborated, *mound builders*. The fact, now well known, that they entered Yucatan with arts nearly perfected and were themselves correspondingly advanced in culture when they came thither from the sea (as they claimed), seems to bear out the supposition that they owed their habits of high foundation building, their many arts almost perfected from the beginning of their occupancy, and to some extent their own origin, to a key-dwelling phase of existence.*

---

*I am not alone in thus having found a decided correspondence between the arts of the ancient Floridians and other Southern Indians and those of ancient Yucatan. Other observers, in particular Dr. Daniel G. Brinton, Profs. F. W. Putnam, William H. Holmes, Frederick Starr and Dr. Cyrus Thomas, have noted unmistakable similarities between the arts of Yucatan and Mexico, and those of the mound builders of the Gulf States. I think it has been held that these arts traveled overland in some way along the far-reaching western and northern Gulf shores from south northward. As I have already stated, however, arts, and especially ceremonial and decorative art forms, do not readily travel from one tribe to another, are not easily adopted by one primitive people from another, unless both peoples are in a very similar grade of cultural development or share a common environment in which these arts are natural and at home. Moreover, it is to be reflected that not only arts, but also peoples (in sufficient numbers to impress their culture

The foregoing more or less speculative conclusions have been offered tentatively, not as final, but for whatever value they may possess as suggestions. After all, the collections and observations under consideration are equally interesting whether these suggestions be true or not, or only in part true. Quite aside from all this, the large proportion of objects in perishable material, recovered by us, renders our collections from the keys unique in one respect at least; serves to illustrate how very little, after all, of the art of a Stone Age people (or in this case Shell Age people) is really represented by the remains that are commonly found on the camp sites and in the burial places of such peoples. Had my collections and observations been confined to the shell, bone, horn, pottery and other specimens in comparatively enduring materials found on the keys, the art that they represent would have seemed exceedingly crude, almost below the average of Stone Age art generally, here in America. As it was, however, the carved and painted works in wood alone, in these collections, served of themselves to indicate that here were the remains of a people not only well advanced toward barbaric civilization, but of a people with a very ancient and distinctive culture, whose relations with other peoples may, through these same rare specimens of their arts—that alone by immersion in the water courts were

---

or arts upon others) travel very slowly by land—impeded as they are in their course if it be long, by tribe after tribe, and danger after danger. But both arts and peoples travel with the utmost facility by sea. Therefore, it must have been, if not by slower derivation through the key dwellers, then by a wholesale sort of intercourse by sea, that these arts of the civilized peoples of Central America came to be so liberally represented among the remains—especially certain ceremonial and decorative remains—of the Indians of our Southern States, if, indeed, they came from so far south northward and were not, as I incline to think, distributed or inherited from some common centre.

In this connection I will mention also, that Prof. Holmes has found probable traces of Caribbean art in Florida. By an examination of the collections gathered by ourselves as compared with those made by Mr. Clarence Moore throughout the eastern half of the State, however, I find that these Caribbean art forms are less characteristic of our collections than of those from the easterly portion of the State, and even from the Atlantic side of southern Georgia. While the art characteristics I am speaking of, chiefly exhibited in the involuted and concentric surface decoration of paddled pottery, may be accounted for as having originated independently both among the Caribbeans and here throughout Floridian areas—from the graining of the wood of the paddles themselves, or of worn-out wooden vessels in imitation of which this pottery was no doubt at first made—still, there is a large degree of probability that the Caribs had more or less impressed their art, and even themselves, upon a portion of the native population of Florida, long before the discovery. This probability is rendered the greater by the linguistic correspondences which Dr. Albert S. Gatchet has clearly traced between the languages of the aborigines of eastern Florida, the Timuquanans, and the Caribs. However, these Carib influences seem to have come into Florida, not by a westerly way, but from the south and the east, possibly through the Lucayos or Bahamas Islands, the inhabitants of which were within historic times, as is well attested by the earliest writers, in continual intercourse with the natives of the Florida Peninsula. Such traces of Antillean art as are found in the region of the ancient key dwellers and further north on the western, or Gulf coast, seem to be rather more ancient than the date of Caribbean occupation, even of the West Indian Islands themselves, that is, they seem to be far more *Arawak* than Caribbean, and this again coincides with the idea of a very far outhern origin (in the beginning) of these peoples of the keys.

preserved to us—be studied in many ways with unusually satisfactory results.

Another feature of these collections, of equal, if not of greater interest, is the fact that they represent a Shell Age phase of human development and culture. Their art is not only an art of the sea, but it is an art of shells and teeth, an art for which the sea supplied nearly all the working parts of tools, the land only some of the materials worked upon. A study of these tools of shell and teeth furnishes us with an instructive lesson as to the ingenuity of primitive man, as to his capability of meeting needs with help of what would at first seem to be impossible, or but very indifferent, means ; and as to the effect of this on derived art in general. The lesson is suggestive. It would seem to indicate that not here alone, or in those more extended regions of subtropic and tropic America which I have mentioned as possibly the homes of like key-dwelling peoples, but that in many further parts of the world—of the Old World as well as of the New World—such a phase of development may well have been passed through by whole peoples who later became stone-using peoples ; yet whose earlier art of the sea had in like manner influenced the art of their later conditions, of their inland descendants and those who came into continual contact with them —just as this art seems to have influenced that of the mound builders and as a similar art—possessing no less striking marks of the sea, seems to have influenced early men in southern and eastern Asia—like the aboriginal Siamese and Cambodians, Coreans, Chinese and Japanese. Nearer parallels yet, may be found among living peoples, as before stated, those of Borneo and Papua and other parts of the Eastern Archipelago, of the Caroline Islands and other parts of Polynesia. The further question is therefore suggested—whether perhaps, in some portions of the world (man having in all probability made the very beginning of his development as a tool-maker upon the food-abounding seashore of some tropic land) whether in the phase of life here exemplified among the keys, we may not (despite its far higher development), find some intimation of the remotest of human beginnings in the use of tools and weapons as made of sea-produced and other *organic* materials. At any rate, since returning from Florida and studying such sea-land remains as I could find in various museums, and in one case studying them in the actual field (on the coast of Maine, this last summer), I have found that teeth and shells, wherever suitable kinds of these natural tools of the animals themselves could be secured, have played a far more important part, even in the arts of peoples who had abundance of excellent material for stone implements at hand, than has hitherto been realized.

There is no subject in the range of anthropological study, and this especially applies to the study of prehistoric anthropology, which can take rank above the subject of ethnographic origins. By this I mean, for the moment, neither the relations, nor the migrations of peoples, primarily, but the study of peculiar arts, institutions, and other cultural characteristics, as influenced by given or specific physiographic areas. As affording a concrete example of this kind, of the interrelation of man and a particular kind of environment, I know of few cases in which the evidences are so direct and pronounced and I may add, unmistakable, as they are in the peculiar art remains which we discovered in this not less peculiar region of the keys.

I have presented not a few illustrations of this influence as giving rise to key building, and some phases of the life itself of the people who built the keys. Yet in closing I wish once more to recur to the subject. In a preceding note, and in former writings (published in periodicals and in the Reports of the Bureau of Ethnology, on the Zuñi Indians, and the ancient Cliff Dwellers, and the development of Pueblo culture in general), I have shown how the desert of our great southwest and the necessity for overcoming there, the difficulties of existence in an arid waste, may account for the high development towards civilization of the peoples who for a long time dwelt there. It is, indeed, safe for us to infer from these and later studies, especially those of Prof. W J McGee, that the very beginnings of true civilization, in the matter, for example, of agriculture, must ever have been made in desert environments more or less like these, more or less, also, in the same manner.

Well, so in other ways it was, in the wild region of sea, the great sea-waste wherein the ancient key dwellers reclaimed and built their homes. It was as truly a desert, not of the dry land, but of the waters, and likewise it both forced and fostered, rapid and high development of the peoples who entered it and elected or were driven to abide in it. That the island homes of these peoples, the shell keys, might be built, and in the ample water courts thereof a constant supply of fish be provided, it was even more necessary, after such beginnings as I have pictured on a former page, for men to unite in each single enterprise ; the which led directly, not only to increased communality, but also to a higher, and in this case, an effective degree of organization. The arid deserts have led men like the Pueblos to continued agricultural effort wherein it was necessary for them to closely unite in the watering or irrigating of the soil ; and concomitantly it has led them to a high degree of architectural development in not only granary-, and house- construction itself, but also in protective building, fortification, against those who, tempted by the ample stores thus garnered, sought to rob them ; and finally, it has led, through these two causes for united effort, to high communal organization and high *sociologic* and sacerdotal government. But the men of the desert sea wastes, here among the keys, were beset by dangers far greater than those of human foemen, necessitating far more arduous communal effort in the construction of places, rather than houses, of harbors and storm defenses, rather than fortified dwellings ; and the construction of these places under such difficulty and stress, led to far more highly concerted action and therefore developed necessarily not only sociologic organization nearly as high, but perforce a far higher *executive* governmental organization.

The development of the key dwellers in this direction, is attested by every key ruin—little or great—built so long ago, yet enduring the storms that have since played havoc with the mainland; is mutely yet even more eloquently attested by every great group of the shell mounds on these keys built for the chief's houses and temples; by every lengthy canal built from materials of slow and laborious accumulation from the depths of the sea. Therefore, to my mind, there can be no question that the executive, rather than the social side of government was developed among these ancient key dwellers to an almost disproportionate degree; to a degree which led not only to the establishment among them of totemic priests and headmen, as among the Pueblos, but to more than this—to the development of a favored class, and of chieftains even in civil life little short of regal in power and tenure of office.

A curious side of their life may be seen to have almost unavoidably helped toward such a development. With agricultural peoples of the desert, beginnings are almost always made normally,—in the totemic or purely clanal condition of development. Thus the lands, the garnered stores and the very houses, belong primarily to the women, and therefore the existence among them of *men* of a highly privileged class—as, of any directly hereditary line of chieftains—is rarely, if ever, fostered. On land, it was not until by the domestication of animals and the wandering pastoral mode of life this involved was adopted, that formal patriarchal or gentile organizations replaced mother right in property and the matriarchal or clanal organization of society and government—since only then did property come to be held by the *men*. For it was not until men held all-important possessions that they took the lead, and by ever-increasing competition in these, ushered in the growth of privileged classes, the establishment of *direct* heredity, and so, of lines of patriarchal elders, headmen or chieftains. But it may be seen that here on the keys the case was different from the very outset. The one most important possession of the key dwellers was the *canoe*. This was essentially a *man's* possession. Thus what on land was effected by the possession (by the men), of herds and beasts of burden, was here in the sea effected by that of an inanimate (but supposedly animate) vehicle of burden, the canoe. While the women stayed at home in the houses of the safe and isolated keys, the men continually went forth over the surrounding waters in these canoes that were owned by themselves. Being the possessors of property so important to the lives of the whole people, here where the plan of social organization was still, no doubt, at least traditionally totemic, it must nevertheless have become to a limited extent patriarchal—virtually so, as far as the ruling class of men was concerned. This property-right of the men, in canoes that were so directly related to the public works which fostered the executive function in government, then, helped, I take it, toward the establishment of king-like chieftainships; and the main point of this seeming digression is, that it was due to this kind of life and development originally, and to inheritance therefrom, that all the great southern tribes encountered by De Soto and his successors, were ruled over by the most powerful chiefs we know of, outside of Mexico, Peru and Central America, anywhere on this continent; namely, the Mikos or King-chiefs, who had actual power of life and death over nearly all—save members of the priesthood—among their subjects, and were held to be of divine descent.

This abnormally high development in government, indicated by great public works on the keys and among the mounds, and in a measure by historic records, is, as we have seen, paralleled in the arts of the keys, for in them we found, along with an exceedingly high growth of the conventional side of art, an artistic freedom on the æsthetic side that I have not seen equaled in any of the primitive remains of this continent, elsewhere, save alone perhaps, in those of Central America. This gives good ground for another generalization; that while the desert of the land, with its scant vegetation and scanter animal life, leads naturally, yet through the technique involved, to *formal* conventional art, the desert of the sea, teeming with growth and quick with animal life in untold variety, beauty and abundance, leads as in this case, and for like reasons, not to formal, but to highly realistic conventionalization. In the one art, that of the land desert, may be found abundant textile and basketry forms of decoration. There, life seems to have been held so dearly that only in angular or geometric style, or by means of pure symbols rather than by direct representation, were animistic qualities *attributed* to things made; so that above any other art, the art of the arid desert may be called *attributive* art. But here in the sea wastes, where life so abounded, the *forms*, alike of animals and of men, were lavishly, most realistically and gracefully represented, and the commonest tools were shaped over with quite unmistakable life-marks and other added features, and were thus, while conventionally, withal realistically and fearlessly *invested*, with their animistic and specialistic powers. So, in contrast to the art of the inland desert, this of the sea may be called an *art of investure*. It seems to me that now possessing as we do examples of these opposite extremes of art (for museums are filled with the one extreme) there is scarcely a primitive kind of art, ancient or modern, which cannot be measurably interpreted by comparative study of the one kind (the conventional and attributive) and the other kind so clearly illustrated by our collection (the realistic and the conventionally investive). In this, then, as in its exemplification of man's direct relationship in cultural and even perhaps in racial development, to his environment, our study of the ancient key remains, takes its place in the general study of the Science of Man.

I have only to add that the combined archæological data and collections which we gathered from the ancient keys, were together so complete (happily because so many perishable objects were preserved intact and in their proper relations) that they might be called, what though so very ancient, almost literally ethnological, rather than archæological collections. The specimens themselves are now sadly warped and shriveled. But happily some of them can be fairly restored by treatment with preservatives ; and happily also, our photographs, drawings and paintings, and casts, made in the field, are almost equal for study to what the originals were when found. Thus, after the original series is arranged and exhibited here in the Museum of the University of Pennsylvania, and after a duplicate but representative series is displayed in the National Museum at Washington, further comparative study of them will be possible, and through this study the ancient key dwellers as a people, the story even of their modes of daily life, will become known to us so fully as to make it almost like unto one which might be told of a living people. And were it possible now, I would fain present a picture of this olden life on our shores—so remotely pre-Columbian and so truly primitive—since I am sure that with the materials at hand it could even now be made more perfect and detailed than any relating to a period equally remote, that has thus far been possible. Certainly it could be so made when aided, not only by comparative study of the works of such peoples as, let us say the Arawaks of Brazil and the Orinoco, but also, of the early historic records. Still, I shall have to content myself—and perhaps it is just as well, since this will give time for carrying the details of such study much further— with presenting a picture of the kind in the final, fully and amply illustrated volume of the Pepper-Hearst Expedition, which Major Powell has so liberly consented—as a joint work of the Bureau of American Ethnology of the Smithsonian Institution, and the Department of Archæology and Palæontology of the University of Pennsylvania—to publish.

Plate XXV, p. 88 : for 351, 354, read 24, 27 ; for 408, 409, 410, read 80, 81, 82 ; for 410, read 81.

Plate XXVI, p. 89 : for 335, 337, read 7, 9.

Plate XXVII, p. 90 : for 331, 350, read 3, 23.

Plate XXVIII, p. 91 : for 338, 341, read 10, 12 ; for 108, 109, read 81, 82.

Plate XXIX, p. 92 : for 338, 339, read 10, 12.

Plate XXX, p. 93 : for 349, 350, read 21, 22.

Plate XXXI, p. 94 : for 350, 356, read 22, 28.

Plate XXXII, p. 95 : for 368, read 40 ; for 369, read 41 ; for 371, 372, read 43, 44 ; for 372, 373, read 44, 45 ; for 365, read 37 ; for 364, read 36 ; for 361, 366, read 33, 38.

Plate XXXIII, p. 96 : for 388, 394, read 60, 66.

Plate XXXIV, pp. 98, 99, 100 : for rivean (p. 98), read riven ; for 384, 385 (p. 99), read 56, 57 ; for 382, 385 (p. 99), read 53, 56 ; for 386, 387, read 58, 59 ; for 393, 394, 402, read 66, 74 ; for Fig. 6, read Fig. 5 ; for 385, 386 (p. 100), read 56, 57 ; for 363, read 35.

Plate XXXV, p. 101, 103 : for 387 (p. 101), read 59, also 71, 72 ; for 89 (p. 101), read 61 ; for 392 (p. 101), read 64 ; for 393, 394, 402 (p. 103), read 66, 74 ; for 373 (p. 103), read 45 ; for 386, 387 (p. 103), read 58, 59 ; for 374, 375 (p. 103), read 46, 47 ; for 375, 388 (p. 103), read 47, 60.

DESCRIPTIVE LIST OF PLATES XXV–XXXV.

WITH EXPLANATIONS OF FIGURES,

AND TEXT REFERENCES.

PLATE XXV.

The outline map, shown on Plate XXV, is reproduced from the latest Government Hydrographic Surveys, and indicates the location of Tarpon Springs,—the northernmost point on the Gulf coast of Florida (see pp. 351 to 354, inclusive), explored by the Pepper-Hearst expedition of 1896 ; also the location of Key Marco and of the contiguous archipelago of the Ten Thousand Islands,—which probably contains not fewer than fifteen hundred ancient key-dweller settlements or artificial shell islets.

It is designed especially to illustrate the relation (discussed on pp. 408, 409 and 410 in the text) of the Currents of the Caribbean Sea to the principal island clusters or settlements of the ancient key-builders, as probably bearing, to some extent on their remote origin. The series of arrows represented as leading past the gulf of Maracaibo, in South America, thence through the strait between Yucatan and western Cuba, and thence in turn, to the keys and islands of southwestern Florida, defines the current, which is regarded as having been influential in peopling these areas of the keys with wanderers—probably of Arawak extraction, *via* the region of the Orinoco in South America.

Again, the series of arrows represented as passing northwardly along the outer or Atlantic side of both the Lesser and Greater Antilles, and thence to the Lucayo or Bahama Islands, defines the current which is regarded as the possible line of comparatively recent Caribbean derivation, as evidenced by various art remains in eastern Florida and Georgia, which are referred to, in the footnote on page 410, as discovered by Prof. Wm. H. Holmes.

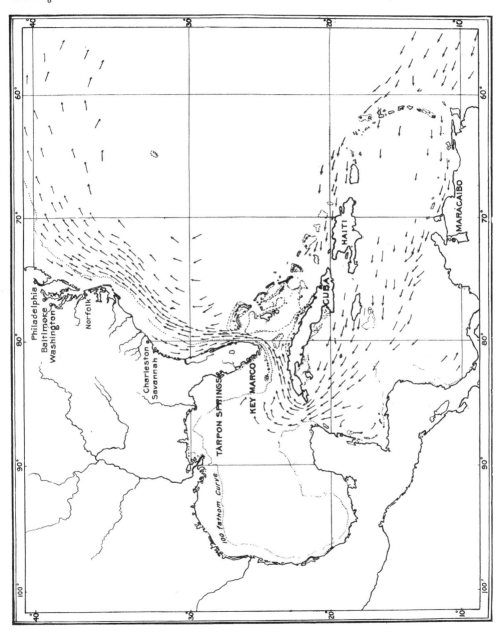

*Location of Ancient Shell Settlements of Key Marco and the Ten Thousand Islands on the Gulf Coast of Florida,
in relation to Currents of the Caribbean Sea.*

PLATE XXVI.

The view presented on Plate **XXVI** illustrates the appearance
of certain shoals and islets to the eastward of Key Marco, in the
northwesterly edge of the Ten Thousand Islands. It admirably exhib-
its the form of an original oyster-bar or coral-reef, as defined by
the lines of foam caused by the rapidly retreating tide. It will be
observed that these lines enclose a central space of deep water (between
the two black masses of reef-crags already exposed), and that these
foam lines extend off laterally, forming an irregular, atoll-like, or
semicircular enclosure, that greatly resembles the outline or plan of a
true, built up or artificial key, or shell settlement.

For this and other reasons—discussed at length on pp. 335 to 337,
inclusive, and incidentally elsewhere in the text—it is supposed that the
earliest key-builders made the beginnings of their great shell structures
or islands (such as are mapped on Plates **XXVIII** and **XXX**) upon reefs
and shoals like these.

The appearance, seen from a distance, of these shell islets or keys, when
overgrown and surrounded by mangroves, as nearly all of them are,
is quite well shown toward the left, and also at the extreme right, of
the picture.

Keys and Reefs among the Ten Thousand Islands, near Marco.

Plate XXVII.

The photograph reproduced on Plate XXVII, was taken from the southern sea-wall of Cayo del Oso, or Bear Key (visible in the leftward distance of the view on the preceding Plate,—XXVI). The outlying portions of this key had been burned over, on the hither side, and although the inner portions were not typically lofty or extensive, nevertheless the marginal structures of the keys in general,—as described on pp. 331 to 350, inclusive—were here exceptionally well revealed. Hence, this view was chosen from among many more impressive scenes, as best illustrating the surrounding enclosures and other details of such keys : First, of the sea-walls, outwardly fringed by mangroves (both seen to the left of the picture) ; of a small fish-pond or water-court with its little outlet-canal seen beyond the second ridge of the foreground) ; and of a larger, partly filled water-court (seen between the third ridge and the western sea-wall —its canal leading off among the trees and bushes to the right). Unfortunately the heights of this key are hidden, or are at best but slightly indicated—in the shrubbery at the extreme right background of the view—giving an impression of flatness that is not characteristic.

Sea-walls and Enclosures surrounding Ancient Shell Settlement at Bear's Point or Cayo Del Oso, of the Ten Thousand Islands;
showing characteristic Fringe of Tidal Mangrove Swamp.

PLATE XXVIII.

In the plan and elevation of Demorey's key presented on Plate XXVIII (described at length on pp. 338 to 341, inclusive), one of the most perfectly preserved, and probably most recent, of the ancient shell settlements or artificial islands of Charlotte Harbor.and neighboring waters is outlined.

The upper sketch-map, although not sufficiently detailed, was drawn from a careful survey laboriously made by myself, and gives a fairly accurate general idea of the terminal terraces, the two inner canals, the principal graded way, the central group of mounds and pyramids, and the great crowning terrace—with its subsidiary platform of approach—as in part illustrated in the succeeding Plate,—XXIX. Unfortunately, however, neither the sea-wall extensions, the nearly submerged enclosures within the swamps, nor the drainage- and garden-basins—or "Spring holes," locally so-called—in the northern benches or low platforms, could be properly shown on this scale.

The subjoined elevation was redrawn from an imperfect sketch of my own taken from the top of a tree, necessarily inside the key, and hence it gives a view-point that does not quite coincide with the more correct orientation of the map above. Nor does it correspond in scale—of details, —hence the central group of mounds appears too far to the right, and the altar-mounds at the end of the crowning terrace are unduly exaggerated in both height and length. Nevertheless, the general contour of the elevations here shown will serve to suggest, in a measure, their striking similarity to mound-groups in the Mississippi and tributary Valleys, and to the terrace-, or platform-builded foundation-structures of ancient Central American cities, referred to in the concluding paragraphs of the text, on pp. 108, 109.

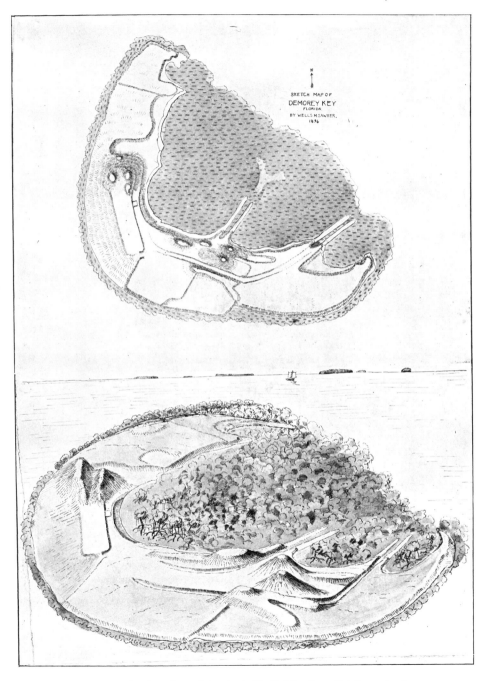

Plan and Elevation of Ancient Shell Island or Settlement of
Demorey's Key, in Pine Island Sound.

PLATE XXIX.

The view of the rounded corner and a portion of the side at the south-eastern end of the shell-faced platform on the crowning terrace or elongated pyramid-mound of Demorey's Key, Pine Island Sound, given in Plate XXIX, does not, unfortunately, include the subsidiary platform of approach at the farther end. As related on pp. 338 and 339, the vegetation covering this and nearly all other portions of the key, was so rank, that but for an accident, the character of the shell work of this terrace would not have been even suspected. Hence too, the tessellated pavement of clamshells along the lines of approach to the side platform and toward the end of the main work, were exposed only here and there, at great labor, and therefore do not appear in the picture. It will be observed however, that the apices of many of the shells in the facing of the terrace, are crushed in. It was found that as this ancient façade was built up, the conches were laid in place—the whorls of each course all turned one way—and that finally all were hammered into place more firmly, until the whole facing was thereby made even. It was thus that the points or spires of some of the shells were broken in as shown. I later learned that this mode of building was resorted to not only in such facings of the heights, but also in the laying of the foundations of the keys on the submerged reefs

Crowning Terrace of the Great Mound or Pyramid on Demorey's Key, showing Platform and Conch-shell Facing.

PLATE XXX.

The contour lines in the Topographic map of Key Marco (represented on Plate XXX, and described on pp. 349, 350, of the text), by means of which Mr. Sawyer has indicated, with the utmost fidelity and accuracy, the minutest features of that remarkable and gigantic structure, necessarily have to be reproduced here in one color. Therefore, the significant difference between elevations and depressions above and below the mean or high tide level are not clearly apparent. For example, the circles and parallel lines in the extreme southeastern portion of the map, represent deep round wells or basins, and almost equally deep canals and graded ways leading to and from them ; while the quite similar, although more numerous, lines at 13', 14' and 18', in the easterly central portion of the map, indicate mounds and other heights above the mean, corresponding, in foot-measure, to these several figures.

The long, narrow water-court or fish-pound—at the northern end—still slightly open to the sea through its short canal ; the three larger courts—respectively twenty, thirty, and fifty feet wide—down on the western side, and the larger triangular "Court of the Pile Dwellers" excavated by us and shown more fully in the plan on Plate XXXI, are all indicated by flat shading, and are marked with mangrove signs.

It will be noted that above and toward the left of this court, are two similar courts, that had been filled nearly up to their marginal rims, probably to form gardens or platforms ; and that to the right, the very large bayou at the southern end of the key was already being reclaimed for the formation of additional courts or enclosures, by the extension of the shell works down toward the terminal eastern sea wall. Excavations revealed the fact that in places the borders of this bayou were already occupied by dwellings like those of the courts, at the time of the abandonment of the place.

The eastern edge of the key was worn away by the sea. The termini of canals similar to those on the northwestern edge, as well as the general oval outline of other portions of the key, indicated that it originally extended a little more than two hundred feet out in this direction, and that it probably here also contained water-courts, fish-pounds and other features, like those lower down on the opposite margin. It also indicated that at the time of abandonment, the place of the extensive mangrove swamp to the southward, was open water, and that the main tidal current between the key and Caximbas island further to the south, flowed past this easterly portion. It is remarkable that Key Marco is exceptional in having thus been somewhat demolished ; for of more than a hundred keys examined by me, first and last, only this and five others had been disturbed by the countless storms that have, throughout unnumbered centuries, swept those regions and changed, on every hand, all other sections of the coast. During the ages that must have elapsed since these gigantic structures were piled up, they have stood unscathed, the stress of tidal wave, and flood and storm ; and they were, in early historic days, as is abundantly attested by old writers, used as places of refuge in times of inundation, by Indians, as, indeed, they have continued to be used ever since, even by modern settlers.

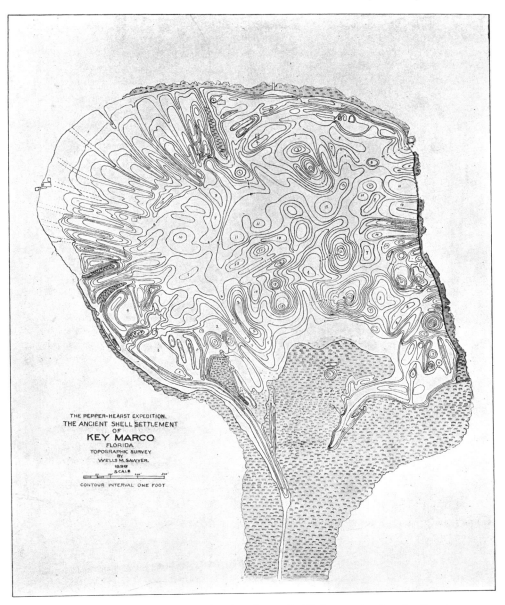

Topographic Map of Key Marco, showing Sea-wall, Water-courts, Canals, Cenotes or Round Reservoirs, Garden-terraces and Central Mounds.

94

PLATE XXXI.

Little more need be said of the Plan and Section of the "Court of the Pile Dwellers" at Key Marco, shown on Plate XXXI, than has already been remarked in the text (on pp. 350, 356, and succeeding pages, and again in the explanations of figures, that follow).

The section below this plan corresponds to an east and west line through the court from above section 1, to above section 70 ; and the heavy black border-line around the margins of the court, represents accurately the area cleanly excavated by us. The locations of preliminary excavations by Collier, Wilkins, Durnford and myself, in sections 14, 23, 32, 33, 34 and 44; those of the shell house-piers and -benches, and those of structural finds and of the inlet- and outlet-canals, are significantly indicated by the dotted enclosures, legends, and graphic figures.

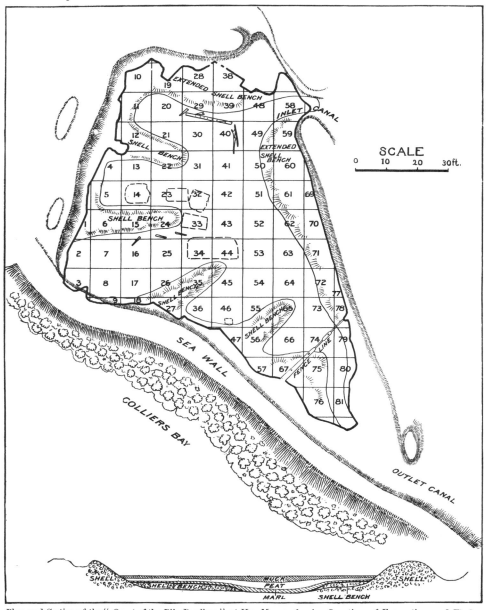

Plan and Section of the " Court of the Pile Dwellers," at Key Marco, showing Locations of Excavations and Finds.

PLATE XXXII.

Only a few typical examples of more than two hundred fairly well-preserved tools and weapons recovered by us from the court of the Pile Dwellers, could here be figured.

Fig. 1. Represents a hafted busycon-, or conch-shell gouge or adze—such as described on p. 368. The length of the handle, which was of buttonwood, was fifteen inches ; of the shell head or armature, seven inches. This particular specimen was found by Gause, close to the edge of the shell bench,—in section 21 (Plate XXXI).

Fig. 2. Represents the handle of a carving-adze of hard, dark wood, like madeira in appearance. It and others of its kind are described on p. 369 of the text. The length of its handle, from end to crook, was twelve inches ; of the head, from the crook down to the insertion of the socketed blade-receptacle of deer horn, five and a fraction inches ; and of this ingenious bit-holder, three inches. It was found with eight other similarly crooked and socketed adze-handles—all contained in a ceremonial pack,—in section 40 (Plate XXXI).

Fig. 3. Represents a superb, single-hole atlatl, described with others, on pp. 371 and 372. It is, by an oversight, figured upside down in this illustration—the tail of the rabbit-carving at the end, having been skilfully adapted to form the propelling spur of this remarkable throwing-apparatus. Its length was nineteen inches, and it was made from fine, springy hard wood—like rose wood in appearance—probably the heart portion of the so-called iron-wood of the region. It was found, associated with the plugged and hollowed or " footed " shaftment of an elaborate cane throwing-spear,—in section 62 (Plate XXXI).

Fig. 4. Represents a double-holed atlatl or spear-thrower. It is described, with the preceding specimen, on pp. 371, 372 of the text, and like it, consisted of dark, red-brown, flexible wood. It was sixteen inches in length, and was found,—in section 29 (Plate XXXI).

Fig. 5. Represents roughly, one of the singular and highly finished hard-wood sabre-clubs armed with shark teeth, which are described on pp. 372, 373 of the text. They were from twenty-four to thirty inches in length, and probably, like the war-clubs of the Zuñi Indians, corresponded to the length of arm, or of thigh from hip to knee, of those who made and used them. The specimen here figured was found by Mr. Bergmann,—in section 11 (Plate XXXI).

Fig. 6. Represents a toy canoe, of cypress wood, nineteen and three-quarter inches in length. As described on p. 365 of the text, it was found with another of like proportions—to which it had been attached, probably in imitation of sea-going catamaran-canoes of the ancient key dwellers, by means of cross-stays,— by Gause and Clark,—in section 26 (Plate XXXI).

Fig. 7. Represents a little flat-bottomed toy canoe, (such as described on p. 364) of the kind supposed to have been used in canals, bayous, and other shoal waters. It was found by myself,—in section 7 (Plate XXXI).

Fig. 8. Represents a paddle of hard wood, the end of handle burned off as described on pp. 361, 366. It was found by Gause, sticking slantingly up through the muck, in the mouth of the inlet-canal,—in section 48 (Plate XXXI).

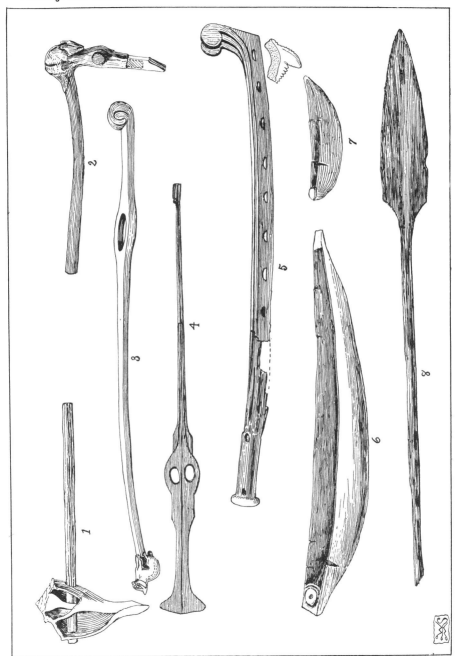

Types of Implements and Weapons ; Toy Canoes and Paddle.

PLATE XXXIII.

Of the many animal figureheads, and actually, as well as decoratively, associated human masks discovered in the Court of the Pile Dwellers, those of the wolf and wolf-man, and of the pelican and pelican-man only, were chosen for illustration here, not because they were the most striking or perfect examples of the kind recovered, but because they illustrate more completely than others, the singular relations and meanings of these peculiar objects of art—as I have endeavored to explain them in the text, on pp. 388 to 394, inclusive.

Fig. 1. Represents very perfectly, the wolf figurehead, as it appears when the parts are put together as the relations of the perforations and cord fragments therein indicate they were originally joined. When this figurehead was found,—by Gause and myself, in section 30, Plate XXXI —the ear-pieces were back to back, and were thrust through the hollow head-piece and open mouth ; and the conventional, scroll-like shoulder and leg-pieces, were laid together in like manner, and were neatly bound, with strips of palmetto, or flag-leaf—still green in color—to the side of the head. This head-piece was six and one-half inches in length ; the spread of the jaws, five and seven-eighth inches ; the ear-pieces, six inches in length, and the leg and shoulder-pieces, four and six-eighths inches long. Happily, Mr. Sawyer was able to make an excellent water-color sketch of the specimen before it was disturbed, and another after it was put together and was still bright with the moisture of its centuries of immersion and preservation.

Fig. 2. Represents the human featured mask associated with this wolf figure-head. It is less perfectly shown in the sketch, since the details of its paint decoration do not, in mere black and white, show as plainly as could be desired, and hence the really unmistakable correspondence between these color-designs (in black, brown, gray-blue and white), and the general aspect and face-markings of the animal-head, is not so pronounced as in the original. But the black ear-marks over the eyes, the black, indented stripe under and around the nostrils, the scroll-like outlines of the shoulder-pieces (in white lines over all the other markings in the middle of the face), and the zigzag lines representative of the gnashing teeth or tusked jaws of the wolf (across the cheeks toward the mouth of the mask), will at once, however, be recognized.

This mask was nine inches in length, by six inches in width, and was found in the same section, (30), not only with the wolf figurehead, but also near other masks and figureheads.

Fig. 3. Represents, on a greatly reduced scale, the pelican figurehead,— found by Gause and Hudson, in section 40. This extraordinarily grace-

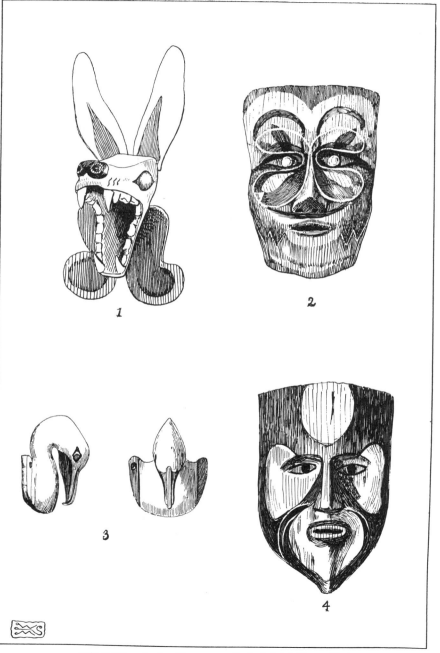

Animal Figure-heads with correspondingly Painted Human Masks.

ful, and realistically painted carving, was four and one-half inches high, by three inches in width of shoulders ; it was much under natural size of the bird it represented, but it was surprisingly life-like, what though so beautifully and conventionally idealized as a figure of the head and front of the pelican. Near it were thin slats, admirably cut and painted to represent the wings of the bird ; and they were pierced, as were the incut shoulders of the figurehead itself, for attachment thereto. The mask (fig. 4) found near this figurehead and the other painted carvings mentioned, was nine and one-eighth inches high, and five and one-quarter inches broad. It was unquestionably designed to represent the human, or man-god counterpart of this bird ; for not only was the chin protruded and the under lip pouted to symbolize the pouch of the pelican, but also, the rear and tail of the body (painted in white on the chin), the trailing legs (in gray-blue and white lines, descending from the nostrils around the corners of the mouth), the wings and shoulders, (in dappled white over the cheeks), and the huge bald head (in white on the forehead of the mask), were all most distinctly suggested. Moreover, on the upper edge of the mask (at the terminal point of the bird head painted on the forehead), were perforations, indicating that either an actual beak, or an appendage representative thereof, had been attached. With this in mind, if the mask be reversed and a comparison of the design on it be made with the figurehead, or with the imagined form of a flying peli-can seen from above, the almost ludicrous resemblance of the design to its supposed original will readily enough be seen.

PLATE XXXIV.

Fig. 1, in Plate **XXXIV**, represents a tablet of rivean cypress wood, shaved with shark-tooth blades to a uniform thickness of less than half an inch,—the characteristic marks of this work being visible all over the unpainted portions of both sides of the board. It was found by myself, standing slantingly upright—in section 21 (Plate XXXI), the painted side fortunately protected by its oblique position. It was marvelously fresh when first uncovered,—the wood, of a bright yellowish-brown color, and the painting vivid and clear. It is sixteen and a half inches in length by eight and a half inches in width, and was slightly concavo-convex from side to side. Upon the hollow side is painted the figure of a crested bird, with four circlets falling from his mouth. A black bar, and over it the outlines, in white, of an animal, is represented as under the talons; and a long, double-pointed object,—probably a double-bladed paddle,—as borne aloft under the right wing of the figure.

The drawing here shown was made from a very obscure photographic print, and does not, therefore, adequately show some of the minutest, yet most significant details visible in either the original or in the fine full sized painting made by Mr. Sawyer when the specimen was freshly taken up from the muck. In the first place, the bands and spaces of white on the figure, enclosed very significant zones of clear light blue, —on the crest, neck, body and wings. They do not show here, but they made it possible to identify this primitive bird painting as that of the *jay*, or else of the *king fisher*, or more probably still, of a crested mythic bird or bird-god combining attributes of both.*

---

*In reference to certain scarred or crest-marked skulls found by us in the burial mound at Tarpon Springs, I wrote the Chief Ethnologist of the Bureau of American Ethnology, Prof. W J McGee, as follows:

"—— ——, it is a well-known fact that certain classes of men among the Southern tribes,—notably those of the Maskokian confederacy, the Creeks especially,—wore the hair in erect crests, cropped and narrow in front, broadening rearwardly to the back of the head, where it was allowed to grow to the normal length, and whence it depended in each case, either naturally like a tail, or bound about with fur or stuffs, to form the so-called scalp-lock. The researches of Gatschet make it evident that this was the special hair-dress of the Warrior-class (see portrait of Tomochichi, a Yamasee war-chief, in Urlsperger, vol. i). He finds that in the Creek language, Tás-sa (Hichiti Tás-si), signifies alike 'jay or king-fisher' ('crested bird') and 'hair-crest;' while Tás-si ka-ya signifies 'Warrior; (lit., 'crest standing up'—that is, 'he of the erectile crest'). From other sources it appears that as the jay was regarded as more powerful in resisting even birds of prey than were any other birds of his kind,—as was also the king-fisher, so nearly resembling him, more powerful than other birds of his kind,—because of their shrill and startling cries and their habits of erecting their hair-like crests when alarmed in defending, or wrathful in offending their kind. Wherefore, the crest of the jay and of the male king-

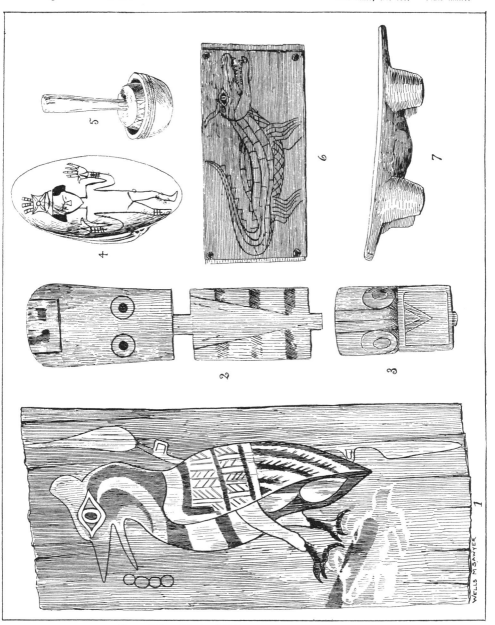

Types of Sacred Painted Tablets and Shell, and of Utensils.

In the second place, all of the main outlines of this primitive painting, —the crest, neck, breast, shoulder, and oblique end of the tail, were delicately spaced, so as to produce the effect of double outlining and so as to enhance both the beauty and the perspective of the figure. The centres of the circlets falling from the open beak were filled with pigment—originally blue, white, and probably red,—and a tongue-like line of white extended from the mouth to the circlets and was oppositely continued in black, into the *throat* of the figure—enabling me to identify it as the heart-line, and these circlets as "living," or "sounding" breaths or words—symbolizing the "commands of the four quarters." The animal represented under the talons of the bird figure, had a long and faintly *ringed* tail, which extended nearly to the lower paddle-blade, and enabled me to identify it, in turn, as a picture of the raccoon—all as more fully described on pp. 384 and 385 of the text.

Fig. 2 represents one of those mysterious objects described on pp. 382 to 385 inclusive, as "altar-", or "ancestral-tablets." It was painted on both sides,—in black and white on the side here shown, and with four round marks of white enclosed and dotted in black, centrally and equidistantly disposed along the other side. It was made of light wood, —pine or cypress,—was two feet three and a half inches high, ten inches wide, flat, and an inch thick below the shoulders, and nearly three inches thick in the middle of convex shovel-shaped head or nose. It seems to be the highly conventionalized representation, as does the little amulet of coral lime-stone below (Fig. 3, which is barely two inches long, by one and a quarter inches wide), of some kind of monster of the deep— like the alligator, or cayman or American crocodile.

Fig. 4 represents the painted valve of a pair of sun-shells described on pp. 386 and 387 ; and compared as to details on pp. 393, 394 and 402, as well as in Plate XXXV, with corresponding mound builder delineations. They were found tightly closed together, and near some symbolic head-slats, on which a bird-god (like the one just described) had been painted, —in section 30 (Plate XXXI), by Messrs. Gause and Bergmann.

Fig. 6 represents a beautiful little pestle and bowl of mastich-wood found together as here shown, although tilted over—in section 40—by Alfred Hudson. The pestle was six and a half inches high ; the bowl, three and a quarter inches in diameter. Both were handsomely polished and were reticularly decorated with incised lines, so delicate as to almost escape detection.

fisher,—who were probably bird-gods of war,—came to be imitated (reproduced, so far as possible) in the head-dress (or aspect) of the Warrior—the Wrathful Defender of his People and their Homes."

I quote this passage, which was later substantially published in the *American Anthropologist* (vol. x, pp. 17 and 18), because I think it throws light on the meaning of the tablet here described and figured, not only as being really a painting of the Bird-God of War of the ancient key dwellers, but also, because of its apparent bearing on probable historic or derivative connections of the Southern Indians with a key dweller people or ancestry.

Fig. 6 represents a little jewel-box lid or bottom, of hard, dark brown wood, eight inches in length, by four in width. The ends were rabbetted and drilled for attachment (with sinew and black gum, traces of which remained), to the ends of the box, and the ends themselves were in juxtaposition. Each end was four inches long and of corresponding width, and painted lengthwise on the outside, with double mythic tie-cords and shell-clasp figures. The bottom and the other parts were missing, save for fragments. With these fragments, however, were some of the most superb ear jewels and plugs, shell beads and pearls, among all our findings. Curiously enough, the remarkable outline of a horned crocodile, painted on this little lid as here shown, occured on the *inside*, and this plainly indicates the sacred nature of the box and its contents. It is of interest to note that the horned crocodile (or alligator) was seen by William Bartram, painted on the façades of the great sacred houses of the Creek Indians, when he visited their chief towns more than a hundred years ago.

This specimen was found by Hudson and myself, with the ceremonial pack and painted shell described on pp. 385, 386,—in section 40 (Plate XXXI).

Fig. 7 represents a stool—described, with others of its kind, on p. 363. It is seventeen inches in length, between six and seven inches in width, and at one end, five, at the other end, six inches high. It was blocked out with shell adzes—as shown by traces of hacking still visible on its under side, then finished with shark tooth knives,—from a piece of hard, yellowish wood, probably buttonwood. It was found by Clark,—in section 31.

I would call attention to the fact that it is sloped, or higher at one end than at the other. This indicates that it was designed for use *astride*, so to say, as is also indicated in other, even unsloped specimens, by the slant of the pegs or feet, which adapted some of these stools for use in canoes, lengthwise, but not crosswise. It is well known that the Antilleans, whose stools, while far more elaborate than those we found, were not unlike them in style, had a fashion of sitting astride or lengthwise of them. While this may, with many other points, signify connection, it far more certainly signifies that this curious way of sitting was established by the use of long stools in narrow canoes, and possibly also, by use of the sitting-hammock.

PLATE XXXV

The first figure here given, represents the statuette of a panther or mountain lion-god. It is six inches in height by two and a half inches in length of base, from heel to knee-bend. It is carved from an exceedingly hard knot, or gnarled block of fine, dark-brown wood, and had either been saturated with some kind of varnish, or more probably had been frequently anointed with the fat of slain animals or victims. To this, doubtless, its remarkable preservation is due ; for it is still relatively heavier, harder, and less shrunken by drying, than any other specimen of like material in the collection.

This extraordinary object of art is generally described on p. 387, and is referred to elsewhere in the text ; but I would again call attention to the fact that while the head and body are not only delicately fashioned and finished, even to the extent of polishing, the legs and the ends of the paws, although smoothed outside, are simply shaped, and,—as though purposely—left unfinished ; and the spaces below the tail—which is conventionally laid along the back after the manner of Zuñi carvings of the same sort of animal-god—and the spaces between the legs, still show the characteristic marks of the fine-edged shark-tooth-blade with which the figure was carved.

I found this gem of our art collections—on a happy day—at a depth of not more than twenty inches, just between the overlying muck and the middle stratum of peat-marl, near the edge of the shell-bench—in section 15. Not far away were found, a large stool, a decayed mask, portions of a short wooden stave, and of symbolic ear-buttons ; a sheaf of about two dozen throwing arrows, and other remains of warrior- and hunter-paraphernalia and accoutrements. This affords convincing evidence that the statuette was a fetish or god of war or the hunt, like its clumsier stone analogues in Zuñi land.

Fig. 2 represents the finest and most perfectly preserved example of combined carving and painting, that we found—unless the figurehead of a great sea turtle and its companion masks, referred to on p. 89, be exempted. In form, or mere contour, it portrayed with startling fidelity and delicacy, the head of a young deer or doe, a little under life-size ; that is, in length, from back of head to muzzle, seven and a half inches ; in breadth across the forehead, five and a half inches. The view, as stated in the text, on p. 392, where the significance of this figurehead is discussed at large,—was an unfortunate choice for illustration, since it is in full front, instead of in profile or a three-quarter aspect. Certain points not noted in the text should be referred to here. Not only were the ears. the bases of which were hollow, or tubular—and as already

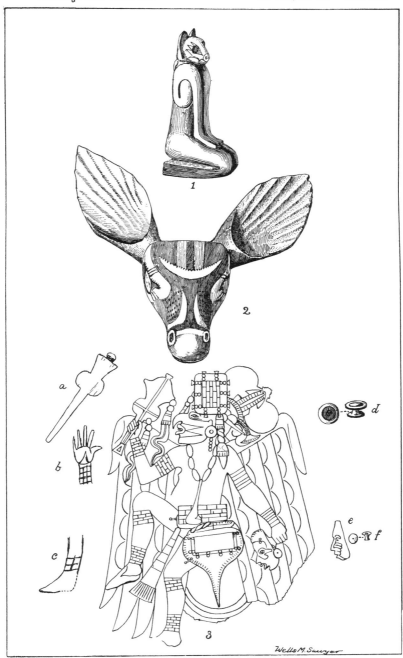

Wells M. Sawyer

Statuette of the Lion or Panther-God ; Figure-head of Deer ; comparison of Key Dweller Types of Ceremonial Paraphernalia, etc., with Delineations on Ancient Copper Plate from the Etowah Mound of Georgia.

stated transfixed with pegs to facilitate attachment by means of cords passed through bifurcate holes at the back edge of the headpiece,—but they were also relatively large, and were fluted, and their tips were curved as in nature, only more regularly ; and they were painted inside with a creamy pink-white pigment to represent their translucency ; and the black hair-tufts at the back were neatly represented by short, double black streaks of paint, laid on lengthwise and close together. On the crown of the head were two slight, flat protuberances, with central peg-holes, for the attachment of small antlers, probably imitative, for they had disappeared, as actual horns would not have done.

The slime of the tortoise-shell eyes still remained in place, and the combined bees-wax and rubber-gum cement with which they had been secured was still intact when the specimen was found. The whites of the eyes had consisted of some very bright gum-like substance, and the front corners or creases of the eyes had been filled with black gum and varnish, highly polished, so that, save for the four conventional sets of equidistantly radiating winker-marks, they gave a surprisingly life-like, realistic and timid or appealing, yet winsome expression, to the whole face. The muzzle, nostrils, and especially the exquisitely modeled and painted chin and lower jaw, were so delicately idealized that it was evident the primitive artist who fashioned this masterpiece, loved, with both ardor and reverence, the animal he was portraying.

The face-markings were perfectly symmetrical. Those in white are sufficiently shown in the drawing. The cheeks or jowls were gray-blue, merging upwardly into black, and the two central and lateral bands over the forehead were divided by a deep black band, and were themselves of a deeper blue. The face, below the forehead-crescent, and between and to either side of the white nose-marks, was painted a dull black ; while the nozzle was covered with an intensely black and gleaming varnish, and the nostrils, which were outlined in black, were deeply cut in and partially filled with a thick dead black substance, to make them appear still deeper.

I need only add that all the face-marks were not only delicately outlined with black, but were edged with fine, regular hair-marks ; and that like marks, as well as minute stipplings, covered all the blue, and lighter black areas of the face and sides, while along, and to the rear, of the upper lip, the hair-warts were represented by neat, oval and regularly disposed, thick or protuberant dots of black gum or varnish.

Although so much of the line-painting on this figure was as fine as though made with a camel's-hair brush, it was evident, as on other painted specimens, that points and spatulæ of some kind—probably of wood—as well as brushes of human hair, had been employed in much of the work ; for the paint was mixed thickly with gum-sizing,—such as we found many lumps of, in several shells filled with both the black kind, and with the less permanent white and blue kinds of pigment.,

Fortunately, we secured an excellent photograph of this splendid specimen, in situ ; and fortunately, also, it was immediately yielded to Mrs. Cushing's care. For she placed it, with a few other choice specimens, in a protected corner of our cabin, turning it and them, carefully, daily, so that they dried so evenly and slowly that they neither warped nor checked—only grew smaller in the process.

Fig. 3,—a, b, c, d, e, and f. The illustration here offered has been so fully referred to in various portions of the text, especially on pp. 393, 394 and 402, that little need be added.

While the central figure represents the art of the Georgia mound builders, the marginal figures (of warclub, a—described on p. 373) ; of plait-bound wrist-band and leg-band (b, c,—both painted in ventral valve of a sun-shell, described on pp. 386, 387 and illustrated in Fig. 4, Plate XXXIV) ; of large, inlaid, eye-like ear-button (d,—described on pp. 374, 375) ; and of mask and ear-plug (f,—respectively described on p. 375 and pp. 388 et seq.), are taken from objects and art specimens found by us in the Court of the Pile Dwellers, at Key Marco. The correspondence between them and the details and paraphernalia of the Georgia figure, is sufficiently apparent at a glance.

It is desirable, however, to indicate several other points of correspondence which might have been as clearly shown, given more ample scope of illustration. In fact, our finds in the keys,—carefully observed in their relations to one another,—actually furnish a nearly complete commentary or explanation, of almost everything portrayed in connection with this remarkable delineation of the ancient mound builders so skilfully rendered and accurately reproduced in Prof. Holme's drawing here given.

To begin with, the war-club we found was *practical*—a war-club for use ; while the baton-like war-club held in the hand of the figure was ceremonial and decorative. Nevertheless, our specimen, like the one in the figure, was furnished with a knob at the end, grooved for the attachment of a tassel, precisely like the other one, conventionally shown in this figure ; that is, the cord of attachment had been furnished, not with two, but with one, sliding-bead (similar beads of both shell and deerhorn were frequently found by us). The node below these beads had been formed by enwrapping a little conical plug of wood lengthwise and then around—in a manner quite familiar to our grandmothers, and shown clearly in the figure before us—and the fringe of the tassel had been made of combined yellow, and green, very finely twisted, sea island cotton cordage.

I have already commented upon the beads of the necklace worn in this figure. The pendant hanging therefrom, represents a typical form found in all the more northerly of the Florida Keys. It is made from the columnella and a portion of the spire of the busy con-conch-shell so common there. These large-headed, pin-like pendants, were not only used as such, on necklaces, but were also favorite ear-spikes and -pendants combined. When worn as ear-spikes, they were thrust through the ears so that the polished conical plate formed from the spire of the shell, showed like a convex disc, in front.

The central portion of such a head-frontlet as is shown turned side-wise over the forehead of this figure, was found by me between sections 20 and 29, near the fine figurehead of an osprey or fish hawk. It consisted, not of four, but of six, slender yellow wooden slats, shaved as thin as cardboard, and lying side by side,—in which position relative to one another, they had been secured by fine threads, alternately woven over and under the slats, precisely as seems to be indicated in this primitive delineation. The slats that I found, however, had been figured over with black paint (and probably other colors), but the design could no longer be made out.

One other feature in this figure deserves interpretation in the light of our finds—the representations of *hair* on various parts of it. On such of our specimens as exhibited hair painting, the mode of representation was precisely such as that exhibited around, (1) the pointed flap at the hip of the figure; (2) on the cross-marked, semicircular band at the back of the head, as well as, (3) in the centre of the object that stands slantingly up therefrom; and finally, (4) on the tail-like tassel stiffly depending from the back of the head, as well as (5) over the crest of the hand-mask held below. All this makes it clear that (1) the flap in question, was that of a beaded and otherwise decorated girdle-pouch of *fur ;* that the semicircular band (2) was a hair-crest, while the object (3) slanting up from it, was an elaborate hair-knot, attached to either side of which was a thin semicircular plate,—in this case, probably, of mica : for among the keys, silmilar, curious plates, were made either of gleaming pinna shell, or of rubbed down, and highly polished pecten shells; while in ancient Shawnee mounds, identical forms have been found, made, however, from the palmate portions of elk horns, and furnished with teeth or narrow combs, unmistakably to facilitate insertion into the hair. Finally (4) the dark tassel is simply a plaited scalp-lock or queue, the end cut off squarely, and the hair standing out, therefore, like the bristles of a much spread brush.

Yet other details in this and kindred figures of mound builder art, could be explained equally well by comparisons with our finds as observed *in situ,* but enough has been said, I trust, to render quite conclusive the close and actual relation, if not the identity, of our key-dweller art, with typical examples like this, of mound builder art—such relation as I have not hesitated to suggest in the text.

DISCUSSION.

DR. BRINTON :

Mr. President :—After the brilliant demonstration of discoveries in an entirely new field of American archæology, to which we have been privileged to listen this evening, all that I could add is a discussion as to the probabilities of the builders of those remarkable remains being known or unknown to us. I shall review, briefly, the history, so far as we know it, and the ethnography, so far as we know it, of the localities in which these were found.

Columbus, in his first three voyages, did not hear of the Northern continent. He struck the Bahamas ; he was in Cuba ; he heard of the Southern continent ; he heard of Yucatan ; but he did not hear, apparently, of Florida. His last voyages were made from what he had learned from the Indians of Cuba as to where the mainland was situated. He went toward the south, as you know, and toward the west. He did not go toward the north. So far as we know the first information which was derived by the Spanish settlers of Cuba and the Antilles —their first information of the Northern continent—came somewhat later. It was probably twenty years afterward that they first made their expedition to discover what is now known as Florida.

The earliest exploration, which was that made by Ponce de Leon, he was distinctly led to make, according to the information we derive from his contemporaries, by reports of the Indians of Cuba. He went very nearly to this spot which has been shown on the map this evening and journeyed northward. What led him, according to the statements, was not only the thirst for gold but a nobler idea, the discovery of the fountain, the river, of perpetual life. It is a common belief, among the North American and South American Indians, that somewhere or other there is that fountain or stream. It can be explained by their general theory of mythology. No doubt it was shared by the Indians of Cuba ; no doubt he heard of that, and it led him, therefore, in part, to make his expedition. He carried it out with unfortunate results, so we have never been able to profit by the discovery in the sense in which he intended it. That was about 1512 to 1520—two expeditions which were sent out by him or under his charge. We have no very full reports of them, although we have some accounts.

On the other hand, we have abundant information of the expedition which was headed by Hernando de Soto, who reached the Florida shore in 1540. He landed also on the west coast of Florida, and probably in Tampa Bay ; most likely near the present town of Tampa. We learn from the accounts of that expedition that he discovered there tribes who were accustomed to build just such mounds as have been described to you this evening. Those mounds are still in existence, and, so far as we can locate the mound-builders, they were precisely where he pointed them out. The historians of his expedition say, "The natives builded their houses on mounds made with hand for strength," as military positions, and in order to raise them above the waters which sometimes invaded them. We have, therefore, a distinct statement, which cannot be controverted, that at that time those people were accustomed to build just such structures as those which have been mentioned to you to-night.

From that time on the sources of our information are rather abundant. There was a Spaniard (one of many who had been wrecked on the Florida reefs) by name d'Escalante Fontaneda, who had been captured by the Indians and remained with them six or eight years, about 1552 to 1560. He lived to write an account of his explorations there. He said he had traveled all over the peninsula of fair Florida, and adds that he "had bathed in every river that he had come to, hoping that it would be the one to confer upon him perpetual life." He regretted to add that he had not found it, otherwise we should have had him here to-night.

He says of the people there dwelling that they "live in a condition of comparative simplicity, but are great warriors and fine archers." He adds that they were divided into a certain series of village communities ; and he mentions one in particular where he stayed the longest time, about the locality described by Mr. Cushing. He gives us the name of the chief of the country, Caloosa ; he tells us also that that had been a kingdom for many generations, and furnishes a few particulars as to the genealogy of the king ; among others, the name of his father (Sequene) and the names of his ancestors. We have, therefore, rather strong evidence from this that the people who constructed these mounds belonged to a race who continued to live there for some time after the first discovery of the country.

From that time on Florida becomes a known country. In 1562, the Protestants, who had been sent out by Admiral Coligny, settled in the vicinity of the lower St. Johns, not far from St. Augustine. They remained there five years ; wrote several very excellent books about it (which we still have, fortunately) ; when they were dispossessed and mostly massacred by the Spaniards who came in 1567. The Spaniards made a permanent settlement.

The French had gone far up the St. Johns River, probably to Lake Okeechobee. The Spaniards explored it quite thoroughly and their priests immediately began to study the languages and write books in them and instruct their converts in religion. We have not all those books, but we have several of them, so that we know something about the native tongues of Florida at that time.

I need scarcely pursue this branch of the subject further than to say that it was probably nearly a century before a Christian (Catholic) church was founded directly in the locality which has been described to-night. It was probably about 1660 or 1666 that the Bishop established a permanent priest there. He did not, however, have sufficient means to extend his parochial duties very far ; so that a chieftain of this very tribe went over to the Bishop of Havana in 1668 and asked for an additional priest. We have the record of that journey. He sent over with this messenger a written description of what he wanted, not written in the Spanish nor in Latin letters, but in characters which they were accustomed to use, somewhat similar, probably, to those four speech-words which Mr. Cushing has shown us to-night on one of these illustrations, some form of hieroglyph.

Now, how can we get at the evidence as to who these people were? We found, in the first place, the earliest discoverers meeting with tribes who lived upon mounds made in the manner described. They are not depicted in full ; but the fact that they were mound-builders and mound-dwellers leads us to suppose that they might have extended to the Florida keys and also the Ten Thousand Islands on the southwestern coast. We have, I take it, the means to a solution through our linguistic studies. Hernando d'Escalante Fontaneda (the Spaniard whom I spoke of, who lived between 1550 to 1560 some five or six years in this very locality) has left us in his memoir some fifty or sixty names of the native towns, villages, chiefs and peoples. They have been very carefully examined by Mr. Buckingham Smith, with the aid of Mr. Pitchlyn (a native Choctaw), and they have, I consider, been practically identified by him as belonging to the Choctaw group of dialects. He has, it appears to me, sufficiently shown this. I will give you two examples out of a number   Fontaneda tells us that one of the villages was called Cuchiyaga, which he translated "The Town of Weeping." Now Mr. Pitchlyn says this means in Choctaw literally, "Where we are going to weep." He gives us the name of the king, Caloosa. There is no doubt that is a Choctaw word. Fontaneda says that it means brave, or fierce, or cruel ; Pitchlyn says Caloosa means "the brave black man," "the brave dark-colored man," dark or black being also the symbol for bravery, boldness, ferocity. We have, therefore, these two words, the meanings of which are given by Fontaneda, and which Pitchlyn says are good Choctaw to-day. I take it, therefore, that there is a very strong supposition that the inhabitants of southwestern Florida spoke a Choctaw dialect.

It is somewhat remarkable that we do not find any French or any Spanish early accounts, giving traces of the Choctaw in the vicinity of the lower St. Johns. That region was populated by an entirely different linguistic stock and people, the Timucuas. Their language has no similarity to any other, either in the Northern or Southern continent. It is absolutely extinct and was a century ago ; but we have, fortunately, one grammar and a confessional in it, which have been lately published by the diligence of several eminent French scholars. We do not find the Timuquanan words on the west coast of Florida, except in the vicinity of Cedar Keys considerably to the north of the locality spoken of to-night.

Mr. Cushing has pointed out a similarity between the cultural elements discovered there and those in the vicinity of the Etowah mounds, where the particular design he showed upon the screen has been taken from. We know that the Etowah mounds were distinctly in the Choctaw country. I believe, therefore, that from the cultural side of the question we have evidence enough to say that the main dialect of southern Florida at the time of the discovery was Choctaw.

At the same time I desire to bring forward some evidence to show that it was not exclusively Choctaw culture. Our very eminent American archæologist, Prof. Holmes, has made a study of pottery throughout western Florida, in which he has shown that the decorations of that pottery are peculiar in character and have many similarities to what he calls the "Antillean culture," or the culture of the Great Antilles— Cuba and so forth. In conversation with him, however, he tells me that all the specimens on which he bases this are superficial finds ; in other words, they lay upon the top of the mounds and village sites and are not ancient. He believes, therefore, that the influence of that culture arrived at a comparatively late period. The explanation of that I believe we can obtain from this same good old Spaniard, Fontaneda. He tells us in his memoir that the natives of Cuba used to come across the Gulf Stream and land in Florida in search of the fountain of life ; and that they came finally in such numbers, that the king, Caloosa, or his father, Sequene, assigned to them a particular village in which they should live, telling them that it was useless to pursue that quest any further. No doubt he had looked for it himself, with disappointing results, and therefore he assigned to them a particular locality on one of these islands, and told them to live there. In all likelihood they brought with them some touches of Antillean culture, which explains the decorative designs of Prof. Holmes.

It is not likely that we can find any trace there of true South American culture. The only people who occupied the Great Antilles and the Bahamas and all the northern portion of the West Indies, were the Arawaks. There has been some question of Caribbean decorative designs ; but the Caribs never extended their permanent settlements even to the island of Cuba. They were known there and Columbus first heard of them there, but they came merely as pirates ; they plundered the shores and carried off women. These Caribs came rather late to the northern shores of South America. They have been traced in the last ten years in a manner which, I believe, is completely satisfactory to American scholars. They never constructed a single permanent village on any part of the North American continent ; never anywhere north of the Isthmus of Panama ; never in Florida or along the gulf. If so, we have no evidence of it whatever ; it has perished utterly. As to the Mayas, Columbus distinctly heard of the Mayas in Cuba ; his attention was called to them by the fact that the Cubans had wax, which they did not make from their native bees. It was the discovery of that wax in Cuba which led him to inquire and to ascertain that it came from the

Mayas at Yucatan. We know therefore that commerce between them once existed ; and no doubt many elements of culture passed over from Yucatan to the western portion of Cuba. We cannot trace it now on account of the total destruction of the Cubans at an early period ; and also because investigations have not been carefully made there for archæological purposes ; but we know the facts ; we know that the Mayas did extend to Cuba, though they had no permanent settlements there. The native languages in Florida—there are really only two so far as the original names are concerned—were the Choctaw and the Timuquanan. In the Antilles, in the Bahamas, and in the whole coast of South America from the mouth of the Orinoco eastward to the mouth of the Amazon, the country was covered exclusively by Arawak vil- lages. They migrated from the south to the north. We can trace them back to the highlands of Bolivia, where their ancestral stock still remains. Their history can be followed linguistically and culturally from the central crestline of South America coming northward. They reached the West India Islands, probably, at no great time anterior to their discovery. It might have been 500 years, or 1000. We have not found on these islands any signs of culture, other than distinctly Arawak or Antillean in character.

It would appear, therefore, from these various lines of argument—his- toric, cultural and linguistic—that we can discern a distinct develop- ment, local in character, ethnic in its traits, of a North American cul- ture. There are, to be sure, many strange points of similarity between that and the Central American and South American culture ; but, as has been said by an eminent American archæologist, "Wherever you find the American Indian, you find him tarred with the same stick." He is always developing under ethnic conditions towards a culture which is similar everywhere. That is shown in many instances where we come to study out any Indian development. Take this one of masks ; if we compare the general character of those masks with those which we find elsewhere (still preserved in actual use) we find a similarity in the traits of them all. American culture is in one sense everywhere the same. It is everywhere the same in its origin and in its lines of develop- ment, although they are deeply influenced by ethnic and local pecu- liarities.

I do not think the culture which has been exhibited here to-night— strange and remarkable and most instructive as it is—has any pecu- liarities which are in themselves broadly distinct from those in the Choctaw district of northern Georgia and in the mounds there. Her- nando de Soto, when about 1540 he made that exploration, found an extremely high state of native civilization throughout northern Georgia. He passed through that region where we find now the Etowah mounds ; he found people there who knew something about the use of gold and silver and who were in what we might call a copper age ; and he encountered a people so highly developed that the his- torians who accompanied him all expressed their admiration at it. The remains which have been discovered since confirm those reports ; so I believe that the culture described this evening, which is eminently a maritime culture, has developed from the same centre, though in its own direction, and has many analogies to the culture which Hernando de Soto found some distance north of it.

We have a record—very unsafe to follow—composed about 1650 to 1658 by an Englishman, written in Latin, translated in French and published in Rochefort's *History of the Antilles,* where the writer says that a general art culture existed from the Appalachean country southward ; and he tells us, as Prof. Mason has pointed out, of dwellings built on piles in the lower portion of Florida. I have not myself examined the original since I saw Prof. Mason's quotation some months ago ; but I think it very likely, that pile dwellings are found anywhere among native tribes where it is convenient to make them. We meet them throughout Borneo and Maracaybo ; and to this day the Seminoles, who live in southern Florida, build their houses often on piles in the bayous. It is one of those natural and necessary methods of construction which we will find under certain geographic conditions wherever they are discovered. This is my contribution to this most interesting study—entirely novel and extremely valuable—to which we have had the privilege of listening.

PROF. PUTNAM :

It is seldom that an archæologist has the opportunity of examining a collection of objects of so much scientific importance as those on exhibition here to-night ; and it is certain that a thorough study of all the results of this exploration, carried on by Mr. Cushing, under the auspices of the University of Pennsylvania, will add largely to our knowledge of American archæology.

Dr. Brinton has expressed the opinion that the people represented by this collection were very likely of the same stock as those in other parts of Florida and Georgia. I fully agree with him on this point, because the culture we have here is of the same type as that known to have existed in other parts of Florida, and in Georgia, and I may say that it is similar to that still farther north, as far up as the Ohio valley.

What I consider the most important point in Mr. Cushing's discoveries is that he was able to bring out of this muck deposit on the Florida Keys a large number of objects which by being buried in the muck were preserved ; whereas the same objects if buried in a sand mound or lost in a shell heap would have perished. It is important to note that the objects in this collection, made of imperishable material, such as stone, bone and shell, are of the same character as those already known from other parts of Florida. Thus it seems to me that Mr. Cushing's discovery instead of indicating a new culture, has thrown a powerful light upon, and greatly extended our knowledge of, the old culture of Florida.

The question we are all asking is, Where did this people originate ?

Mr. Cushing is inclined to believe that they came from South America. I understand that would be your idea (turning to Mr. Cushing), that these were the Arawaks or the Caribs, and that they came up from South America?

MR. CUSHING (answering) : Yes.

PROF. PUTNAM (continuing) : Dr. Brinton is rather inclined to say that they did not come from there.

DR. BRINTON : Because there is no linguistic evidence to that effect.

PROF. PUTNAM : And also that the culture is somewhat different from either the Arawak or the Caribbean. It seems to me that it certainly is a different culture. And now there is another point that we must consider. Mr. Cushing's collection includes a large number of human skulls which I have had the pleasure of seeing in the museum to-day. I am much interested to note that these skulls are of the same type as those found in the sand mounds of Florida. The first of this type that I ever saw came from the sand mounds around Cedar Keys and were brought to notice by the late Prof. Jeffries Wyman. Mr. Clarence B. Moore has found this type in the sand mounds of eastern Florida. The same general type has been found throughout northern Florida, Georgia, Alabama, and through the region extending towards the Cumberland valley in Tennessee ; also westward through the Pueblo region and in Central America. It is the general brachycephalic skull ; not only brachycephalic, but decidedly rounded, with more or less artificial flattening of the frontal and occipital regions. I have regarded this type of skull as belonging to the southern and southwestern peoples of North America. I believe that this type of skull is the type of the people who first settled, so far as we know, in Central America and on the shores of Peru and northern South America; that in all probability this people extended eastward, coming across the Isthmus through the Central American region and extending along the Gulf of Mexico and over into Florida, and finally, judging from the evidence that Mr. Cushing has presented to-night, being driven onto these keys. In fact I should consider it probable that the line of migration was directly opposite to the one which has been suggested. That is, I believe it more likely that this was a people who, having had an early home in the Central American region, extended around the Gulf to Florida, rather than a people who came from South America to the Florida Keys and then spread into Florida and westward.

For a number of years Mr. Clarence B. Moore has been engaged in exploring the sand mounds of Florida. He has found a large number of objects of the same character as many of these upon the table. He has not found any wooden carvings ; I think he has not found anything made of wood except a few very small pieces with copper attached ; but nearly all the bone implements, many of the bone ornaments, and many of the shell implements which are upon the table are almost identical with those found in the sand mounds on the eastern coast of Florida. Thus we find the same culture, so far as the bone and shell objects can determine the question, which existed here on the southwestern coast of Florida, extending northward up the eastern coast.

The wooden objects in this collection are very remarkable ; and the fact that wooden vessels took the place of pottery is an important one, as it seems to indicate that the people were forced to use wood instead of pottery from the abundance of the former and the absence of clay to make the latter. These masks I consider the most marvelous archæological evidence that has ever been brought out. Never before have we been able to dig up masks and to read the story that they tell as Mr. Cushing has read it to us to-night. We know that the people of to-day in Central America use masks very similar to these ; and I believe that the people of South America have somewhat similar masks. We know that many of our Indian tribes have masks of very similar character. This form of mask having the characteristics of the bird, or some animal, represented over the face is so common to-day in Alaska and other parts of the northwest coast, that it is actually startling to an ethnologist to see these masks, dug up in Florida, showing the same character of art. The interpretation that Mr. Cushing has given to this idea of expressing the animal upon the human face and of making the Bird God, or the Wolf God, is the same as that worked out by Dr. Franz Boas ; and this we know to be true from actual evidence of the Indians themselves.

I can only add that when I read Mr. Cushing's first statement of this very interesting discovery, I did not know what to make of it. It seemed to me almost beyond belief that so much of importance could have been found down there in Florida, where so many had been working. From his statement and from the photographs which he has shown us to-night I am satisfied that he has entered upon a very rich field, and one of the utmost importance to the archæology of North America. I sincerely hope that his work will be continued, that he will have an opportunity to return to this place, and, if possible, to work for several years about these keys. This whole subject should be investigated in a thorough manner, that we may understand still more of this people who built these peculiar and wonderful shell structures. We do not begin to appreciate the probable antiquity of this people until we stop to consider that these Florida keys could not have supported a very large population, and that it must have taken an immense amount of time and millions upon millions of conch shells to make these great mounds, upon which the dwellings of the people were probably erected. Mr. Cushing states that this people must have lived upon these keys many centuries (I am inclined to say many thousand years) ago.

There has been presented to us to-night one of the most important archæological papers that I have ever listened to ; and certainly the objects illustrating the paper are of extraordinary interest.

I sincerely congratulate Mr. Cushing, as well as the University and all connected with this expedition, on the important results of his labors.

MR. CUSHING : If I may be permitted, Mr. President, to follow an address, already so long, with a few remarks in reply to the most interesting discussion with which Dr. Brinton and Dr. Putnam have at once honored me and added greatly to the value of my communication, I shall much esteem the privilege.

THE PRESIDENT :—The Society will be pleased, I am sure, to listen to further remarks from Mr. Cushing.

MR. CUSHING :—First, then, in reference to Dr. Brinton's part in the discussion, let me say that it was quite impossible for me to undertake to review, much less to dwell upon, the numerous historic references to early natives in Florida, that seem—as I am well aware—to have pertained to the waning days of a people who were either the actual key dwellers—as I have called them—or were certainly inheritors, in great part, of their culture. Could I have done this, Dr. Brinton would have perceived that my belief fully,—almost more than fully—accorded with his own, regarding the affiliations of these people with later and historic peoples. I would add, relative generally to the early inhabitants of western, southern-central and southwestern Florida, that from archæologic evidence alone, one can scarcely doubt they were, at the time of the discovery, chiefly Maskokians (or of the stock to which not only the Muskhogees, but also the Choctaws or Chahtas, the Hitchiti and other tribes of the Creek Confederacy, of the Southern States, belonged,—as, if I remember aright, Dr. Brinton long ago pointed out in one of his published works. And since I regard these Southern mound-building Indians as having inherited their mound-building habits and much of their culture otherwise, quite directly from key dwellers, I of course believe, with him, that the key dwellers themselves may be looked upon as having been, during the later centuries of their existence, not only American Indians, but North American Indians, and thus, in a racial sense, by no means a new people.

After all, the chief significance of these discoveries and finds of ours in the keys of southwestern Florida is to be found, as I have said before, in the unique illustration they afford of a peculiar local development in culture and art as influenced by, or related to, a peculiar environment ; and in this, while they may not pertain to a new or hitherto unknown people, they certainly do reveal either a new *phase* of human culture, or else an old culture in an entirely new light.

Nevertheless, I wish to explain a little more explicitly, quite exactly where I stand with regard to these ancient key dwellers of mine—as to who they were more remotely, as to what may have been their origin ! It is true I do not believe—and I do not think I have anywhere stated the belief—that they were a *new people,* or even that theirs was wholly a new culture. I admit that there have appeared various articles in which the most extravagant announcements have been made relative to my Florida discoveries,—such announcements as I would not for a moment have encouraged the statement of ; and even in what I myself have written for the press, I cannot be held responsible for "headings" or "editorial leaders,"—much less for comments thereon in the press at large.

But I would repeat that I think a close study of many objects in our collection reveals decided trace of survival in art-types of a kind which cannot be accounted for as well otherwise, as by supposing it to have been derived, inherited remotely, I should say, from farther southern regions—from South America, in all probability. In my spoken address I did little more than touch upon this important point, in order merely to bring it before you in the proper connection, and I may not have stated clearly enough that I did not think the key dwellers themselves, or as a people, were wholly South American. I think, however, that they may have been such in the very beginning ; that a South American people, or that an intermediate sea-dwelling people derived thence, and coming at last on the currents of the Caribbean Sea, to the region of these keys—as indicated by my map—initiated, in this region, the practice of the key building of which I found so many evidences. I have already referred to the pointed paddle we found, which is both South, and Central American, in type ; to the absence of bows, and the presence of atlatls, which are likewise at home in those remoter regions, more so than in these : and to the type of war club which prevails down there, and of which, in particular, I would, even at the risk of repetition, say a little more in this special connection. Let me exhibit to you the actual specimen we found. It is, as I was at considerable pains to show you, Maskokian in type, of the southern mounds ; or, as Dr. Brinton has assured you, Choctaw, which is practically the same thing. But the specimen I hold in my hand is an actual weapon, not merely ceremonial, as were those of the Southern Indians, and it is distinctively South American in type. It is not, save in semblance, such as its parents were. It is wholly of wood, yet it does not represent survival from a club of wood alone. It represents, if I am not mistaken, survival from a form of weapon like the double-bladed battle axe, peculiar, originally, to South America—a form derived from a type of stone-bladed implement nowhere represented in North America. I here refer to the short, broad, and round-bitted, flat-backed celt-blade, sharply notched at the sides near the butt,—not grooved as are the axe blades of the United States,—which anciently prevailed all through the Bolivian Highlands, in Peru, Ecuador and along the upper reaches of the Amazon, and thence spread, no doubt, not only northwardly into the Isthmus, but also northeastwardly down the Amazon and the Orinoco. These blades were set oppositely, not into, but *against* the sides of their club-like handles, and were attached thereto by means of criss-cross bindings alternately passing through the right notch of one blade, obliquely across the handle, and through the left notch of the other blade, then through the right notch of the second blade, again across the opposite side of the handle, and through the left notch of the first blade, in such wise that a weapon exactly resembling this one, in general outline, was produced. From such a form of weapon the double, semicircular bladed battle-axe of copper or bronze which prevailed at the time of the Conquest in both Peru and Isthmean, or Meridian America, appears also to have been derived ; as well as the form of club I have described and here shown to have been almost as characteristic of the keys (and, ceremonially, or still further derivatively, even of the southern mounds) as it was originatively, of the country of its nativity, namely, South America.

Much of like import may be said of the plaited leg-bands represented on the human figure painted in the shell I have exhibited and described. These bands are drawn as passing around,—not the ankles, as at first sight appears,—but around the legs, just below the knees and above the calves ; and we know that both the Arawaks and the Caribs had the curious practice of tightly bandaging the legs in this fashion, in order, it is alleged, to enlarge the calves ; but whether this is so or not, we see that the practice was typically South American ; and I may add that it prevailed nowhere in Northern America except apparently here among the keys and in the mound region, and that in this last, it was evidently a survival ; for it may be seen that the mound plates, such as I have shown you by illustration, represent figures wearing not only wristlets and leg-bands, as in this painting,—and as worn by the South American and Antillean Indians,—but also, armlets or bands *above* the elbows, and anklets or bands *below* the calves, as worn by so many central North American Indians, when first encountered.

Now I have mentioned these comparatively inconspicuous characteristics, not simply because they are the only evidences that might be adduced in support of my supposition, but because they are the readiest at hand and the most easily illustrated, of many such evidences.

I have not been unmindful of the fact that Prof. Holmes pointed out, some years ago, an apparent Caribbean element in the decoration of certain ancient Floridian potteries, and although I surely referred to the subject in the course of my address, I evidently did not make its significance as clear as I trust my published notes will render it. Meanwhile we are certainly off of debatable ground when we study or consider the collections of pottery made by us in the northerly portion of the State, —at Tarpon Springs,—or those made by Mr. Clarence Moore in easterly portions of the State (as compared, in various ways, with the collections of corresponding wooden-ware vessels gathered by us from the southern keys) in reference to their relationship to primitive art-technique and symbolism ; as influenced by, and inherited from, a given environment.

The forms of these terra-cotta vessels, and particularly the decorations upon many of them, were eloquent of at least one thing,—that their types had originated among a people who had once,— ignorant of pottery-making,—made their vessels of shells, of simple gourds, and of wood ; and that those primitive vessels of theirs had been more or less like unto these, their later vessels in clay. For, by critically examining the peculiarly involuted and concentric designs on so many of them, such as were recognized by Prof. Holmes as analogous to Caribbean decorations, I find that they were undoubtedly derived from the natural markings of the curly- or crooked-grained wood of which these ancient peoples had earlier made their principal vessels—that is, before they became makers of pottery vessels at all.

Again, what lends plausibility to this supposition, is the fact that in much of the pottery under consideration the surface-decoration resembles a hachuring—so to call it,—the origin of which is as unmistakably traceable to the surface markings of wooden objects carved with shark-tooth blades ; and is simply the reproductive or imitative perpetuation, in clay materials, of such markings as were unavoidable in vessels thus made of the wood materials that preceded the use of, and served as the models for, these vessels so differently made of pottery materials. All this would, to my mind, indicate that these forms of decoration,—Antillean as well as Floridian—owed their origin to a similar condition and environment,—and thus very probably were derived from some common source.

I failed, it now appears, to consider sufficiently these and many other points which have been so appropriately brought forward and emphasized by Dr. Putnam as well as by Dr. Brinton, because, as I early stated, it seemed necessary for me, in order the better to exhibit and explain the large number of lantern slides (there were sixty-seven of them) to abandon my manuscript notes. From the scientific standpoint I ought not, in justice to my subject, to have done this, and I now regret that I did ; for in the outline or syllabus of the address which I furnished to both Dr. Brinton and Dr. Putnam these points were at least indicated ; and in my manuscript, as will appear when it is fully published, nearly all of them were fairly set forth.

If, then, you will permit me to restate my conclusions on one or two only, of the more general of these points, which seem to me to include or imply so many of the others, I will not detain you longer.

I cannot express too strongly my belief that there was a large " Muskhogian " (or Maskokian) element among the ancient inhabitants of western Florida—so large, in fact, that I think we may justifiably map the whole western half of Florida, to as far south as the very end of the peninsula, as *Maskokian.* Now the Maskokians were mound builders, and therefore, according to my theory, must long have been dwellers in the land. Whether they had themselves come from the South, or whether they came thither from the North, or whether, as has seemed to me more probable, they resulted from an intermingling here of stocks from both directions, these questions still remain, I think, to be determined principally by further archæologic researches of precisely the kind of which I have given you some account this evening,—although much more extended, for I have but entered the borderland, as it were, of an enormously large and fertile field. But I must reiterate that in the keys, in the essential features thereof, and in the principal structures thereon, we have prefigured, as it were, the mound-groups and their outworks—those built not only by the Maskokians and other historic Indians, but also by the prehistoric so-called mound builders themselves ; and since the keys thus represent a kind of mound building that was absolutely essential, while to account for the almost equally laborious earth-mound works, practical necessity cannot be conceived of as a primary cause, I have claimed, not that the mound builders were as a whole derived from the particular key dwellers I have been describing, but that mound building as practiced by them, was derived from an analogous sea-, or shore-land environment. And thus, too, I have ventured to. suggest that the resemblance between the mound-groups of our own land, and the foundation-groups of ancient Central American cities—the plans of the principal structures of which are so strikingly like even the plans of the earlier key structures—may indicate that these, no less than the mound-groups themselves, were developed (with much else in ancient Central American culture) from an original sea environment of the same kind. So, the main point of all I have brought forward in relation to our discoveries and collections as representative of the ancient sea dwellers, is this : That for the study of *beginnings*, alike of the sort just named, and in technology and art, they are exceedingly suggestive and in some respects quite sufficiently conclusive.

In thanking the distinguished gentlemen who have so honored me with their discussion and in thanking the members of this Society for their patient attention throughout, I wish once more to acknowledge my profound appreciation of the aid and encouragement I have received from your distinguished Vice-President, Dr. William Pepper ; my gratitude also to Mrs. Phebe A. Hearst, and to other members of the Board of Managers of the Archæological Association of the University of Pennsylvania, who made possible the investigations of which I have given you account this evening. Had they not thus come forward, I had personally missed an opportunity of enriching my experience in American archæology and ethnology that I have come to feel I could ill have afforded to spare.

[Since the remainder of this discussion consisted chiefly of a detailed description (occupying nearly half an hour) of the specimens and illustrations displayed in the Hall of the Society, I have not hesitated to incorporate the substance of the stenographic notes of it that were kindly furnished me by the Secretaries of the American Philosophical Society, in the body of the published address.

In justice as well to my two distinguished critics, as to myself, however, I must repeat that in the off-hand address which alone they discussed, I may not have made—probably did not make—a number of the points they consider, as clear from my side as they were in my written notes, and as I trust they now are in the fuller text. Hence, it is not only appropriate, but seems to me a duty, to here furnish comments on three or four of these.

Regarding Dr. Brinton's reference to the mounds on Tampa Bay, I find, from the notes of the discussion, that I did not give the subject sufficient attention. I should have stated more fully, that the mounds which have been identified as those discovered by De Soto, were of precisely the kind I have described as occurring on Pine Island. That is, they are not true keys, for they are situated on the mainland, and they are composed of earth and shell combined, as were all the mounds near the gulf coast of Florida that I have described as probably the works of the descendants or successors of the key dwellers proper. True typical shell keys, no fewer than five of them, occur along the Manatee, below the opposite or southward side of Tampa Bay, but these are quite certainly not the mounds referred to as occupied at the time of De Soto. They are either islands, or contiguous to islands. Nevertheless one of them was apparently connected with a later series of earth-works which seem to have been subsidiary, like those of Pine Island, Naples and the Caloosahatchee region. It was in the region of these latter, and of the Okeechobee, that the renowned Chief Sequene and his successors, rulers over the Caloosas, held sway, and it was principally among these people—far inland, and more than a hundred miles northeastwardly from the Key Marco region, that Fontaneda seems to have lived. That the particular peoples mentioned by him were not the same as the key dwellers proper—certainly not the same in period and degree of development—may be inferred from the single fact that they were, as Dr. Brinton quotes, "fine archers;" whereas, I have shown that the true key dwellers were not possessed of the bow at all, but used atlatls and throwing arrows instead, and were not unacquainted, apparently, with the blow gun,—both, I may remark, distinctively South American types of weapon. That they derived these and other things already described, from the Arawaks of a period sufficiently remote to allow time for their domestication—so to say—in this region, still seems to me probable.

While there is much to indicate the comparatively recent introduction into both the Antilles and Florida of the Caribbean element, it seems to me almost certain that if, as is generally affirmed, the Arawaks were the true aborigines of the Greater Antilles, then they must have reached those islands much more anciently than Dr. Brinton is inclined to allow, —for some of the cave remains already found there give positive indication of high antiquity. Again authorities disagree as to the linguistic evidence of Antillean—Carib and Arawak—connection with the natives of southern Florida. An impartial examination of published and unpublished vocabularies convinces me that there is quite as much to prove such connection as has been brought forward to prove Maskokian connection, the number of correspondences between the Arawak and the Timucua and between the Timucua and Maskoki, being, for example, about equal, and quite as readily explicable in both cases on the score of acculturation or borrowing, as on that of descent. It is for this reason that I have regarded archæologic evidence on this question of connections, as equal to, and in some ways superior to, linguistic evidence; and a combination of the two kinds of testimony as superior to either. When, for instance, we find that the same word in both Carib and Timucua signifies not only "Fish-pond" but also "Vegetable garden," and when we consider this in connection with the evidence I discovered on all the ancient keys, of the actual filling in of fish-ponds or enclosures to form of them vegetable gardens, it seems to me we have quite strong indication of a wide-spread practice, commonly derived, by all these peoples.

If the linguistic evidence relative to connections either toward the north or toward the south, of the ancient key dwellers, is thus far so scant as to be inconclusive, this is to a certain extent also the case with the evidence afforded by the human remains we collected. In justice to Dr. Putnam I must state here that the series of skulls in my collections, examined by him, were not the key-dweller skulls. They were skulls derived from the Anclote region, and like those he mentions as previously collected by Dr. Wyman and Mr. Clarence Moore, were exhumed from sand mounds. The true key-dweller skulls found by us in the muck beds at Marco and in the bone pit on Sanybel Island, number only thirteen, but they are pronounced to be, by Dr. Harrison Allen, who is studying them preparatory to full publication, uniformly distinct from those of more northerly and easterly parts of Florida. In the first place, the occipital foraminæ of these remarkable skulls are abnormally large and remain *open* in even the most mature of them,—a characteristic seen in only one cranium of our northern series. In the second place, a curious feature of all these key-dweller skulls is that in no case is the occiput flattened. Finally, they are found to be more nearly of the Antillean type, judged, it is true, by only one or two specimens of the latter examined by Dr. Allen, than of the northern Indian type.

In connection with this, it is significant that the skulls of two dogs, in our collections from the muck, were commented upon by the late Prof. Edward D. Cope, as apparently, almost certainly, skulls of the species of dog common in Incan times to the Peruvian and Bolivian Highlands.

Likewise in justice to Dr. Putnam, I must again state here that while there *was* pottery not only on the terraces, but also in the muck deposits, of the keys, even of the southernmost keys I examined; still, the specimens I exhibited before the Society—three in number—so closely resembled the wooden objects of the same general kind, also exhibited and in greater number, that they may well have been mistaken for vessels of wood unless particularly dwelt upon. It is a curious fact that of all the pottery discovered by us actually in the muck deposit of

Key Marco, only tray-shaped vessels, and either shallow, or hemispheri-cal and deep, sooty, cooking-, or heating bowls of black earthenware, were found. Nearly all, as was to be expected, were crushed; yet from among the numerous sherds carefully saved in lots, Mr. Bergmann and I have succeeded in bringing together the parts of not fewer than fifteen examples, of various sizes; and we hope to restore yet others. One small, shallow bowl, a fragment of which I exhibited to the Society, has happily been almost completely restored. It contains a quite thick mass of black rubber gum—intermixed with crushed shell and other substance—of precisely the kind that was used for cement and paint material as described in the text. Other and larger examples contain almost equally thick coatings of partly charred food, inside, and like all the rest, incrustations of soot, outside.

No relics found by us in the muck so completely evidenced the use of the water courts in which the deposits occurred, as places of actual residence, as did these fire-vessels.

Only a single ornamental fragment was found. This was the conventional figurehead of a crested bird, quite such as is found on many of the traylike bowls of earthenware from the ancient mounds of the Mississippi valley. But it had been drilled and reshaped, to some extent, to serve as a weight or pendant. On the contiguous heights, however, and on the heights of nearly all the keys, especially towards the North, I collected many examples of more elaborate, more decorative and varied pottery, much of it so distinct, in truth, from the pottery of the muck, that I was somewhat puzzled to explain it as the work of the same people, at least in the same period of their development; and, indeed, it may be that in part this pottery of the heights *is* later, and even perhaps represents to some degree the work of later peoples.

I can only add here more deliberately than was possible, of course, in my spoken address, an expression of my continued appreciation of the kindly comments with which Dr. Brinton favored me, and with which Dr. Putnam both opened and closed his discussion.]